£9.95.
JK
(Fow)

0069999

G

THE NATIONAL
CURRICULUM

D1495100

ore

This book is due for return on or before the last da

7.76 37

Kogan Page Books for Teachers series
Series Editor: Tom Marjoram

IMPLEMENTING THE NATIONAL CURRICULUM

The Policy and Practice of
the 1988 Education Reform Act

W S Fowler

Books for Teachers
Series Editor: Tom Marjoram

KOGAN
PAGE

For Jill, Tony and John

First published in 1990 by Kogan Page Ltd
120 Pentonville Road, London N1 9JN

Typeset by DP Photosetting, Aylesbury, Bucks
Printed and bound in Great Britain by
Richard Clay, The Chaucer Press, Bungay

British Library Cataloguing in Publication Data
A CIP Catalogue record for this book is
available from the British Library.

ISBN 0–7494–0208–3

Contents

Preface

One of the first acts of the newly elected Conservative Government of 1987 was the implementation of the educational policies which had been outlined in a White Paper entitled *Better Schools*. A principal plank of these policies was a complete overhaul of the curricular framework of the nation's schools. One month after the General Election, the new Secretary of State for Education and Science issued a detailed introductory document under the title of *The National Curriculum 5–16: A Consultation Document*.

From that moment the pace of the proposed reforms accelerated with dramatic speed. The Education Reform Act was put before Parliament in November 1987 and passed into law eight months later. A major feature of the Act was the introduction of a National Curriculum which became progressively obligatory in all maintained schools from September 1989.

This book charts the progress of the concept of the National Curriculum, a progress which finally crystallised into legal obligations after a two-year snowstorm of consultations, directives and circulars from the DES and the newly established National Curriculum Council.

Included are details of the implementation dates of sections of the National Curriculum, the subject attainment targets at the various age levels for the core foundation subjects, and a discussion of the managerial and other implications of the National Curriculum for heads, teachers, parents and school governors.

Extracts from official material are reproduced with the permission of the Controller of Her Majesty's Stationery Office.

Chapter 1

The Background

The concept of the National Curriculum

The concept of a common or national curriculum may be said to have received its initial ministerial impetus with James Callaghan's speech on education at Ruskin College in 1976. Until the 1970s, governmental interest in education had been largely confined to questions of bricks and mortar, the supply of teachers and major organisational issues, such as the introduction of comprehensive schooling and the right to free higher education. It must also be remembered that it was not until 1972 that the school leaving age was finally raised to 16 years.

An attempt to invade what was known as the 'secret garden' of the curriculum had been made in 1962 with the establishment of a Ministry of Education Central Curriculum Study Group. This group was virtually strangled at birth by the united opposition of the teaching profession, the teacher unions and the local authorities. Two years later the Central Curriculum Study Group was replaced by a national 'representative' body under the title of The Schools Council. This new council was funded jointly by the local education authorities and the DES with the twin aims of assisting schools to plan detailed curricular criteria and overhauling the examination system which was seen as a major obstacle to comprehensive curriculum reforms.

The return of a Labour Government in 1964, however, prompted an immediate and prolonged swing of the searchlight away from curriculum thoughts and towards the organisational problems implicit in the introduction of comprehensive schooling at a national level.

Thus, even as late as 1972 Margaret Thatcher, as the new Education minister, contented herself in *A Framework for Expansion* with addressing the Government's thoughts to the resource problems associated with raising the school leaving age to 16, the question of nursery provision for under-fives, and the manpower requirements implicit in a proposed improvement in school staffing standards.

It was left to the Labour Government in 1976 to renew the 1962 search for the key to the 'secret garden'. This renewed curriculum initiative was heralded by James Callaghan's famous Ruskin College speech. The Prime Minister called for the introduction of a 'Great Debate' on the national aims and needs of education: the time had come for a national curricular consensus to be sought after and achieved. Following the Ruskin College speech the Great Debate itself was launched the following year by the new Education Minister, Shirley Williams. A series of regional conferences was held; these were hosted by the DES and composed of representatives from right across the education spectrum. The 'first thoughts' which resulted from these conferences were codified in the form of the Green Paper of 1977 entitled *Education in Schools: A Consultative Document*. The Green Paper covered a wide range of educational issues and in particular gave a first floating to the concept of some form of *common core curriculum*.

Three years later, in 1970, with a Conservative Government now in power, the Great Debate issues were re-opened by Mark Carlisle, then Secretary of State at the DES, in a consultative document entitled *A Framework for the School Curriculum*. This was the first in a series of three central documents which carried the message that because of the continuing existing diversity of practice in schools, the time had come to prepare guidance on the place which certain *key elements* should have in the experience of every pupil.

The trilogy of documents was careful to stress the important and continuing role of the local education authorities and it asserted that each education authority should prepare clear and known plans for a national curriculum.

The *Framework* papers went as far as to name the subject areas which should form part of a 'core' curriculum — these were identified as science, mathematics, modern languages, religious education and physical education. Furthermore, the papers went on to suggest that approximately 10 per cent of the school timetable would need to be given to these core subjects, in order to achieve worthwhile results.

The following year, in a paper entitled *A Recommended Approach* (DES, 1981), the Government outlined in greater detail its ideas on specific areas of the primary and secondary curriculum. However, it stressed the point that neither the Government itself nor the local education authorities should specify in detail the curriculum of the schools.

In spite of the promptings occasioned by the curriculum papers of 1980 and 1981, the tempo of progress remained, in government terms, disappointingly slow. It was not until 1984 that a more interventionist approach was signalled by the new Secretary of State in the person of Sir Keith Joseph. Speaking at the North of England Educational Conference, Sir Keith announced definitive governmental plans for a complete overhaul of the school curriculum structure. Sir Keith declared that it was the Government's intention:

(a) To define the objectives of the main parts of the 5–16 curriculum so that everyone knows the level of attainment that should be achieved at various stages by pupils of different abilities;
(b) To alter the 16+ examinations so that they measure absolute, rather than relative, performance;
(c) To establish, as a realistic objective, the aim of bringing 80–90 per cent of all pupils at least to the level which is now expected and achieved in the 16+ examinations by pupils of average ability in individual subjects; and to do so over a broad range of skills and competences in a number of subjects.

As examples of the Government's thinking Sir Keith also outlined what he regarded as the proposed minimum levels of attainment at age 16. Thus:

In English, pupils would need to demonstrate that they are attentive listeners and confident speakers when dealing with everyday matters of which they have experience. That they can read straightforward written information and pass it on without loss of meaning, and that they can say clearly what their own views are.

In mathematics, that they understand, and can apply, the topics and skills in the foundation list proposed in the Cockcroft Report.

In science, that they are willing and able to take a practical approach to problems involving sensible observations and appropriate measurements, and can communicate their findings effectively, that they can put information to good use in making sensible predictions from the regularities and patterns which they perceive, and that they can act on instructions presented in a variety of ways and can follow safety procedures.

Although Sir Keith was speaking in 'subject' terms as far as the attainment of objectives was concerned, he nevertheless laid stress upon the underlying principles which should govern the overall structure of the curriculum. In planning an overall curriculum, four principles needed to be observed:

First, it should be broad for all pupils both in the development of personal qualities and in the range of knowledge and skills to which pupils are introduced. That means, for example, that every primary pupil should be properly introduced to science, and that secondary pupils should not drop subjects in the fourth and fifth years in a way which leaves them insufficiently equipped for subsequent study or training.

Second, the curriculum should be relevant to the real world and to the pupils' experience of it. Judged by that test, HMI reports show that much of what pupils are now asked to learn is clutter. The test means, for example, that the curriculum should contain an adequate practical element and promote practical capability for all pupils, not just for those who are labelled 'non-academic'; that the technical and vocational aspect of school learning should have its proper place, and that all pupils should be introduced to the economic and other foundations of our society.

Third, there should be differentiation within the curriculum for variations in the abilities and aptitudes of pupils. This is a task that has to be tackled within each school as well as between schools, where this is relevant.

Fourth, the various elements of the curriculum need to be balanced in such a way as to optimise the contribution that each can make to the total education of the pupil. In so far as each main element does something for the pupil that no other element does, or does as well, no pupil should miss the chance of getting out of each such element the special competence and understanding which it helps him to acquire.

The programme which Sir Keith had outlined in January 1984 was translated into practice with the publication of a major DES White Paper under the heading *Better Schools* in 1985.

This paper outlined the Government's intention to proceed with a wide range of educational reforms. Top of the list were the details of the proposed curriculum changes and these were to be allied to further work on the examination system, action on the problems of discipline and truancy, and new proposals concerning the involvement of parents in the schooling system.

The 1985 White Paper was to mark the end of a lengthy period of discussions by the political parties on the possibility and desirability of some form of common core curriculum which could be adopted at a national level and it heralded the definitive central action which was to occur two years later.

The 1987 Education Reform Bill

In the summer of 1987 the Conservative Government of the day went to the polls. Their election manifesto contained specific references to proposed major reforms in the curriculum, which had been outlined earlier in the year by the new Secretary of State at the Department of Education and Science, Kenneth Baker.

Baker emphasised that the way forward in education must be through 'a national curriculum which works through national criteria for each subject area of the curriculum'.

Following the Conservative election victory the DES lost no time in issuing a major document — the 'red book' — under the title of *The National Curriculum 5–16* (July 1987). This consultative document made the following two principal assertions:

1. All children were entitled to the same opportunities wherever they attended schools.
2. There was a pressing need to raise in 'absolute' rather than relative terms, the overall standards of achievement in the nation's schools.

In order to achieve these goals the Government proposed the establishment of a core curriculum which would be followed by all schools throughout the statutory schooling period of 5–16 years. In primary schools this core curriculum, composed of English, mathematics and science, would occupy the principal amount of teaching time.

Complementing the core curriculum a number of other 'foundation' subjects would be studied by all pupils. These foundation subjects would consist of technology, history, modern languages, geography, art, physical education and music. Taken together it was suggested that the combination of core and foundation subjects would occupy at least 70 per cent of the overall school timetable.

It was further proposed that progress in the three core subjects should be monitored by nationally prescribed tests which would be marked by teachers but moderated and assessed externally.

The establishment of curriculum Working Groups

The consultation document allowed a three-month consultation period on these radical proposals, and during this period comments to the Secretary of State from the outside world ran into thousands of responses. Parallel with this consultation process, the DES announced its intention to set up curriculum Working Groups to prepare detailed programmes of study for two of the core subjects, namely science and mathematics. (Action on defining the core content in English was to be deferred until after the publication of the report of the existing major enquiry on this subject, known as the Kingman enquiry.) In letters to the chairman of the Working Groups, the Secretary of State asked for detailed programmes of study for the core subjects, including content, skill and process elements. Additionally, the Working Groups were asked to provide specific *attainment targets* which pupils of differing abilities might be expected to reach by the end of the school year in which they reached the 'key' ages of 7, 11, 14 and 16.

The Working Groups were to provide interim reports by the end of 1987 and in order to establish a consistent framework for these groups, the Secretary of State appointed, at the same time, a Task Group with the remit of producing general guidelines on assessment and testing procedures.

Simultaneously, the Government pressed ahead with its promised Education Reform Bill and this was presented to Parliament on 20 November 1987. Eight months later, on 29 July 1988, the Bill received Royal Assent and the Government's educational intentions passed on to the Statute Book. During the passage of the Education Reform Bill, remarkably few amendments to the curriculum sections of the Bill were made to the Act itself. The only significant alteration lay in the incorporation of religious education into the framework of the National Curriculum. This important amendment was incorporated into the Act as follows:

1. All pupils at maintained schools must take part in an act of collective worship on each school day.

2. The arrangements for the collective worship may provide for a single act of worship for all pupils or for separate acts of worship for pupils in different age groups or in different school groups.

3. The arrangements for collective worship in county schools and voluntary schools are to be made, in the case of county schools by the headteacher after consulting the governing body and, in the case of voluntary schools, by the governing body after consultation with the headteacher.

4. The act of collective worship in maintained schools must take place on the school premises.

5. In the case of aided, special agreement schools and grant-maintained schools, if the governing body considers that it is desirable for an act of collective worship to take place on a special occasion elsewhere than on the school premises arrangements may be made to do so.

6. In the case of a country school the collective worship must be wholly or mainly of a broadly Christian character, without being distinctive of any particular Christian denomination.

7. In connection with religious education as a required part of the National Curriculum, this education is to be in accordance with the agreed syllabus arrangements. Additionally it will be the duty of each local education authority to constitute a standing advisory council on religious education. This council will have the duty of advising the authority on matters connected with religious worship in county schools and the religious education to be given in accordance with the agreed syllabus.

8. Agreed syllabuses must reflect the fact that the religious traditions in Great Britain are, in the main, Christian, whilst taking into account the teaching and practices of the other principal religions represented in Great Britain.

Chapter 2

General Considerations and the 1988 Act

The parliamentary importance of the Reform Act

In its final version the Education Reform Act contained a total of 238 clauses and gave the Secretary of State 182 new powers. The Bill was debated for a total of 203 hours in the Commons and 150 hours in the Lords, thus becoming the longest piece of parliamentary business since World War II.

In constitutional terms the Act differed markedly from its great reforming predecessor: the Butler Act of 1944. This had been a parliamentary 'consensus' Act, whereas the Baker Act of 1988 contained very strong elements of Conservative party policy. Political agreement on major national educational issues did not appear in any feature of the Act: a factor which prompted commentators to remark that the 'reforming' features of the Act had been designed for political effect rather than educational advantage.

The financial cost of the Reform Act

The total costs involved in the implementation of the Education Reform Act have been variously estimated. Thus the Association of County Councils calculated that the final figure would be in the region of £600 million. Of this figure it was thought that capital expenditure would amount to £200 million and recurrent expenditure would total £400 million. With specific reference to the needs of the National Curriculum, the Secretary of State's Task Group for Testing and Assessment commented that as much as £20 million might be needed to provide a one-day course for every teacher, where supply cover was involved. By 1990/91 it was thought that this overall cost was likely to reach £33 million.

THE COST OF EDUCATION AND THE GROSS DOMESTIC PRODUCT (GDP)

It is worth noting that the total national expenditure on education for 1988/9 was approximately 20 billion pounds. This equalled the total cost of defence for the year and was exceeded by three billion pounds in the case of the Health Service. By far the greatest expenditure was incurred in the sphere of social security which stood at 51 billion pounds. Transport costs accounted for five-and-a-half billion pounds and five billion pounds was spent on law and order.

Thus the total 'cake' of approximately £527 billion was divided as follows:

	Billion
Social security	£51
Health services	£23
Defence	£20
Education	£20
Transport	£ 5.5
Law and order	£ 5
Others	£42.5

The National Curriculum Council: its general and longer term remits

The duty of finalising and disseminating the work of the individual subjects of the new National Curriculum was delegated by the terms of the Education Reform Act to a new body, which was to be known as the National Curriculum Council.

The Act set out the functions of the National Curriculum Council as follows:

(a) to keep all aspects of the curriculum in maintained schools under review;

(b) to advise the Secretary of State on such matters concerned with the curriculum for maintained schools as he may refer to it or as it may see fit;

(c) to advise the Secretary of State on, and if so requested by him to assist him to carry out, programmes of research and development for purposes connected with the curriculum for schools;

(d) to publish and disseminate, and to assist in the publication and dissemination of, information related to the curriculum for schools;

(e) to carry out such ancillary activities as the Secretary of State may direct.

In general, the function of the Council consists in keeping all aspects of the curriculum for county, voluntary, grant-maintained and maintained special schools under review. As part of the review the Secretary of State would expect that he would receive advice from the Council.

It is important to note that the Council's responsibilities are regarded as including religious education, matters relating to the ethnic and cultural diversity of society, the implications of ethnic origin and gender, and also those with special needs: *this overview of the Council covers all aspects of the curriculum, not just the National Curriculum.*

DETAILED DUTIES
Detailed duties of the Curriculum Council were further specified as follows:

1. Training needs for those engaged in the education service (ie teachers, advisers and governors):

   (i) what is the best way in which in-service training can be organised in order to meet the needs of those responsible for implementing attainment targets and programmes of study and assessment in mathematics and science during the first year (starting September 1989). Furthermore, how should the training be organised in the following years?

   (ii) What are the immediate in-service needs, especially of teachers, which will arise from the first 'orders' made in relation to the core subjects of mathematics and science. How can continuous assessment be linked with INSET in relation to the content of what is taught in schools?

   (iii) What training needs to be given in the use of standard assessment tasks which relate to the 'core subjects'. How will the moderation of teachers' assessments be achieved?

Long-term advice on the curriculum

In view of the Curriculum Council's responsibility for keeping the whole curriculum under review, the Secretary of State further asked the Council to consider:

   (i) *The framework of the primary curriculum:* The progressive introduction of the National Curriculum, with its associated assessment and testing arrangements, into primary schools from September 1989 represents a special and immediate challenge because the attainment targets and programmes of study for the core and other foundation subjects need to be set in the context of the primary curriculum as a whole. A start towards understanding that context has been made by the sub-group, chaired by Professor Norman Thomas, which was set up by, and in support of, the first subject working groups. I look to the Council to take that work forward, and to report progress to me by 31 December.

(ii) *Cross curricular issues which should be included in the curriculum of all pupils in maintained schools:* In the first instance that advice should cover the Council's views on the extent to which those issues can be reflected in attainment targets and programmes of study for the core and other foundation subjects, and the place and content of personal and social education, including health education, in the curriculum. The Council is to report progress on these matters by 31 March 1989. Thereafter I shall want the Council similarly to advise me on the place and content of other important cross-curricular issues such as careers education and guidance, and economic awareness.

(iii) *Particular issues related to the final key stage:* The last two years of compulsory schooling — which should be taken into account when introducing the requirement, for fourth-year pupils from September 1990 and the fifth-year pupils from 1991, that the core and other foundation subjects should be studied for a reasonable time. The Council is to advise me on this by 31 March 1989. I shall subsequently look to it for advice on issues which should be taken into account when attainment targets and programmes of study are implemented for that key stage.

Government confidence in the National Curriculum

By 1989 the Government felt confident that public and professional opinion had veered towards acceptance and support for the National Curriculum proposals. Thus, speaking at the North of England Education Conference on 6 January, the Secretary of State remarked:

I first outlined my plans for the National Curriculum to a North of England Conference at Rotherham two years ago. The weather and the reception on that occasion were fairly frosty; and during the subsequent public debate before and after the general election some remarkably censorious things were said — seldom by me. Teaching staff of the London Insitute of Education, for example, said that the National Curriculum framework had so little to commend it that it brought into disrepute the very concept of the common curriculum for the nation's schools. One described the National Curriculum as 'a folly of unprecedented proportions'. And another said that it was hard to see all this resting intact 'under the critical barrage which it has already undergone and may be expected to suffer in the next few months'.

Today the mood has profoundly changed. Successive reports on aspects of the National Curriculum have appeared and been recognised as solid pieces of professional work. Professor Black's report on tests and assessments; the reports on English by Sir John Kingman and Professor Cox; Mr Graham's report on mathematics; Professor Thompson's report on science; and Lady Parkes' report on technology — each in turn has elicited respectful comment and triggered off constructive debate. The *Guardian* — not always enthusiastic about the Government's education policies — wrote of the Cox report on English: 'The ship is moving in the right direction. Ministers have every right to feel satisfied about a difficult job well done'. *The Economist* has recently said that, instead of Britain looking abroad to find cures for our ills, other countries are looking at us to see how they can emulate our success. The Professor of Education at Cambridge has now said that my policies are not radical enough.

Progress report on the National Curriculum

Early in 1989 progress on establishing the National Curriculum and the roles of the Working Groups and National Curriculum Council were summarised by the DES as follows:

1. The Education Reform Act 1988 has established a *National Curriculum* comprising English, mathematics, science, technology, history, geography, a modern foreign language, music, art and PE, and in Wales, Welsh.

2. The function of the *National Curriculum Working Groups* is to advise on the knowledge, skills and understanding ('attainment targets') which pupils should be expected to have acquired at the key ages of 7, 11, 14 and 16, taking account of differences in ability. The groups will also advise on the essential content ('programmes of study') which should be covered to enable pupils to reach the agreed attainment targets.

3. The mathematics and science Working Groups submitted their final reports to the Secretary of State on 30 June 1988. In the light of the Groups' recommendations the Secretary of State produced proposals in August, which have been the subject of statutory consultation by the *National Curriculum Council (NCC)*.

4. The NCC reported to the Secretary of State on 30 November, and he sent out draft orders for mathematics and science for the further process of consultation required under the Education Reform Act 1988 before Christmas 1988. It is expected that the Orders in final form will be laid before Parliament in late February/early March, with implementation for Key Stages 1 and 3 scheduled for September 1989 and for Key Stage 2 in September 1990.

5. In November 1988 the English Working Group submitted its report to the Secretary of State for Key Stages 1 and 2, which was then passed to the National Curriculum Council in November for consultation. It will report on Key Stages 3 and 4 by April 1989. Implementation for Key Stage 1 will take place in September 1989 and for Key Stages 2 and 3 in September 1990. The Working Group considering design and technology submitted its interim report in November 1988 and will submit its final report in April 1989; implementation in the first three key stages will proceed from September 1990. In all cases attainment targets and programmes of study will subsequently be extended to Key Stage 4.

6. *From September 1989 pupils in the firt three key stages will be required to study the foundation subjects of the National Curriculum for a reasonable time* — that is, a time sufficient for each pupil to undertake worthwhile study that contributes towards the provision of a broad and balanced curriculum that helps to prepare them for adult life. The requirement to study a modern foreign language will not apply to pupils in Key Stages 1 and 2.

The National Curriculum in practice

As illustrations of the classroom situations which might evolve from the operation of a national curriculum, the Permanent Secretary at the DES gave two examples. Thus he observed that in the case of *science*:

> Children in the age range 11 to 14 will have to study electromagnetism. They will also have to study everyday applications of magnets and electro-magnets in devices such as electric motors, dynamos, compasses, transformers, sparks, loudspeakers and fuses. They will have to design and make things incorporating magnets and electro-magnets.

Similarly, in the case of core subject *mathematics*:

> One of the mathematics attainment targets will be to recognise and understand percentages. A possible test of that is to ask children to examine attendance rates at school. The task is carefully chosen. It relates directly to the children's experience. But it also requires a good deal of practical effort — for example in planning the survey, gathering the data and analysing the results. Such an exercise can lead straight into the problems of sample surveys and probabilities. This is an example of the way in which the National Curriculum will ensure progression in each child's education — each new challenge building on what has been learned before. (*DES News*, 6 February 1989)

Similarly the Secretary of State used the example of a primary school

23

project on travel to illustrate the type of work which he believed the National Curriculum would encourage further:

> The pupils wrote letters to sponsors, travel agents and friends. They practised using an index and scanning material to find what they really needed. The teacher used the project to extend vocabulary, to teach the proper structure of paragraphs and to improve spelling and syntax. They produced factually accurate writing and also imaginative stories and poems.

Curriculum principles

At the same time, general curriculum principles were re-stated by the Government. It was observed that curricular structures and the core and foundation elements would need to be considered in the light of the necessity for:

1. Continuity and progression throughout the period of compulsory schooling and beyond.
2. Breadth and balance.
3. Relevance: the content and teaching of the various elements of the National Curriculum should bring out their relevance to and links with pupils' own experience and background and their practical application and continuing value to adult and working life.
4. All elements of the curriculum should contribute to the development of general personal qualities and competences in young people which will be of value to them in adult and working life — for example, self-reliance, self-discipline, a spirit of enterprise, a sense of social responsibility, the ability to work harmoniously with others, and the ability to apply knowledge and use it to solve practical real-life problems.
5. It will be important to bear in mind that the curriculum should provide *equal opportunities for boys and girls*. The curriculum should also take account of the ethnic diversity of the school population and society at large.

The role of the attainment targets was also summarised. Thus:

> The attainment targets are expected to provide specific objectives so that pupils, teachers, parents and others have a clear idea of what is expected, and to provide a sound basis for assessment and testing. They should allow scope for the very able, those of average ability and the less able to show what they know and can do. It should not be necessary, particularly for

pupils in the first two key stages, to have different attainment targets for children of different abilities. The targets should be capable of assessment at a range of levels and challenge each child to do the best that he or she can. They should raise expectations, particularly of pupils of middling and lower ability, as well as stretching and stimulating the most able. Working Groups should give particular thought to the application of attainment targets to lower attaining pupils and those with special educational needs.

In the sphere of *special needs*, curriculum Working Groups were reminded that:

The Education Reform Act 1988 provides that where a pupil has a statement of special needs under the 1981 Education Act, the statement should specify any National Curriculum requirements which should not apply or should be modified for that individual pupil. In addition, orders or regulations under the 1988 Act can define the cases or circumstances in which the application of the National Curriculum provisions may be modified or disapplied for any foundation subject.

The Task Group on Assessment and Testing (TGAT)

Crucial to the success of the National Curriculum were underlying concepts of assessment and testing presented by this task group, which had been set up alongside the core curriculum Working Groups in 1987.

The remit of the group was to produce *general* assessment guidelines which could underpin the recommendations of the core and foundation subject working groups. In its preliminary observations the Task Group was at pains to point out that:

1. Its recommendations would be designed to take full account of the good practice and professionalism which already exist generally in schools.
2. The assessments should be *formative*, ie capable of giving helpful information about the possible *future* progress both of individual children and a whole class.
3. At the 16+ level the assessment should also be *summative*, ie provide a record of the achievements of the pupil.
4. *Attitudes* of pupils should not form part of the assessment and testing procedures.
5. The tests should not be *comparative* in nature, ie they should not relate to an outside 'norm' or have reference to averages of performance in a standardised way.

25

6. The tests should give an indication of *each pupil's performance* and therefore the test framework would need to describe clearly the performance which is being expected.
7. A *balance* between precision and detail on the one hand and overall grouping of the ideas, understanding and achievement in the core and foundation subjects would be necessary.

SUBJECT PROFILES

The assessment and testing plan put forward by the Task Group recommended that, in the light of the considerations above, each subject of the National Curriculum should consider up to four sub-divisions of its subject matter: these sub-divisions should be termed *profile components*.

ACHIEVEMENT LEVELS

The Task Group proposed that a ten-point 'scale' should be introduced with the aim of recording the *range of progress* which children might achieve during the age range of 5–16 years. It was suggested that:

1. Each point of the scale should represent the 'average progress' which children might make over a two-year period.
2. Level 1 would always be the starting point of the subject profile element, regardless of the age at which the element was introduced.
3. Children would progress through the 'levels' regardless of their chronological age. Thus in any given age-grouped class of children, some individuals would be working towards higher levels than others.

CHRONOLOGICAL AGE AND ACHIEVEMENT LEVELS

The Task Group recommended that levels 1–3 would cover the likely achievement results for the majority of seven-year-old children.

Similarly, most 11-year-olds could be expected to reach achievement levels 3–5, with some children reaching achievement level 6.

For 14-year-olds, the range would be likely to stretch between levels 4–7.

For 16-year-olds the levels would be matched, after further task group work, with the levels of the new General Certificate of Secondary Education (GCSE) examination.

The relationships between chronological ages and achievement levels were also illustrated diagrammatically by the Task Group as shown in Figure 1.1.

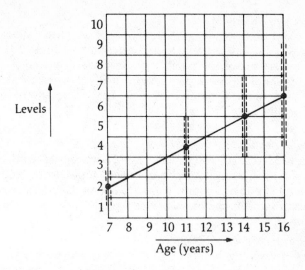

Figure 1.1 *Sequence of pupil achievement of levels between ages 7 and 16*

(The bold line gives the expected results for pupils at the ages specified. The dotted lines represent a rough speculation about the limits within which the great majority of pupils may be found to lie.

The intention is that only the first three levels will be used for most seven-year-olds. Level 1, whether in one profile element or across several, will indicate that a child needs more than ordinary help if he or she is to make satisfactory progress. Level 3 will also signify the need for special provision, but this is because the child is moving ahead quickly. There is no supposition that children in Levels 1 or 3 must be educated outside classes for their own age group. It is expected that the overall national distribution across these three levels will show the large majority of pupils in Level 2. The need to use Levels 1 and 3 may occur more in some profile components, such as learning to read, than in others, such as art.

It is anticipated that the performance of nearly all 11-year-olds will fall in Levels 3, 4 and 5 although a small percentage will have progressed to Level 6 while others, hopefully very few, may not yet have reached Level 3. At 14 the majority of pupils are likely to be spread across four levels. Further work is to be done on how the upper levels match with GCSE grades.

[From: *National Curriculum Task Group on Assessment and Testing Report: Digest* DES, 1988])

METHODS OF ASSESSMENT

The Task Group recommended that final assessments should be reached as a result of a combination of externally set tests combined with the assessments of the pupils' own teachers. The *design of the external tests* should include 'paper and pencil' work, practical work and oral discussion. Examples of such tests were given in the appendices of the *TGAT Report*.

Assessment at the primary school levels

At the 7- and 11-year old assessment stages, it was suggested that, for the most part, the tests should be based on 'topic' work, and that teachers should be able to choose from a 'bank' of material so that the importance of familiar contexts was not neglected.

Children with special educational needs

The Task Group recognised the problems which would face all those concerned with the educational progress of children with special needs. Thus in the report it was noted

> like all children, those with special educational needs require attainable targets to encourage their development and promote their self-esteem. Wherever children with special educational needs are capable of undertaking the national test, they should be encouraged to do so.

Furthermore

> a special unit within a chosen test development agency should be dedicated to producing test material and devising testing and assessment procedures sufficiently wide ranging and sensitive to respond to the needs of these children.

AGREED OUTLINE OF PROCEDURES FOR ASSESSMENT AND TESTING

These recommendations of TGAT were subsequently approved in general terms by Parliament, and Kenneth Baker announced in June 1988 that statutory arrangements would be based on the following points:

1. Attainment targets will be set which establish what children should normally be expected to know, understand and be able to do at the ages of 7, 11, 14 and 16 years; these will enable the progress of each child to be measured against national standards.

2. Pupils' performance in relation to attainment targets should be assessed and reported on at ages 7, 11, 14 and 16 years. Attainment targets should be grouped for this purpose to make the assessment and reporting manageable.
3. Different *levels* of attainment and overall pupil progress demonstrated by tests and assessment should be registered on a 10-point scale covering all the years of compulsory schooling.
4. Assessment should be by a combination of national external tests and assessments by teachers. At age 16 years the GCSE will be the main form of assessment, especially in the core subjects of English, mathematics and science.
5. The results of tests and other assessments should be used both *formatively* to help better teaching and to inform decisions about the next steps for a pupil, and *summatively* at ages 7, 11, 14 and 16 years to inform parents about their child's progress.
6. Detailed results of the assessments of individual pupils should be given in full to parents, and the Government attaches great importance to the principle that these reports should be simple and clear. Individuals' results should not be published, but aggregated results at the ages of 11, 14 and 16 years should be so that the wider public can make informed judgements about attainment in a school or LEA. There should be no legal requirement for schools to publish such results for seven-year-olds, though it is strongly recommended that schools should do so.
7. In order to safeguard standards, assessments made by teachers should be compared with the results of the national tests and with the judgements of other teachers.

It was recognised that a great deal more practical work remained to be done on detailed procedures for the implementation of the national testing and assessment system, and that the first formal published results at the seven-year-old level would not be produced until the summer of 1992.

Timetable for the introduction and assessment of the core and foundation subjects of the National Curriculum

CORE SUBJECTS

Academic year 1989/90
The National Curriculum implementation timetable commenced in the

autumn term 1989 with the publication of draft Orders governing the attainment targets for mathematics and science (for Key Stages 1 and 3) and English (for Key Stage 1). Furthermore, from autumn 1989 it became mandatory for all schools to spend a 'reasonable' amount of time on the National Curriculum foundation subjects. (*Key Stage 1* relates to the 5–7 age group and *Key Stage 3* relates to the 11–14 age group*.)

Academic year 1990/91

In the autumn of 1990 the attainment targets for Key Stage 2 for the core subjects of mathematics, science and English become operative. At the same time attainment targets for technology for Key Stages 1–3 will be introduced.

No *assessment tests* will be introduced until the summer of 1991. At this date, *unreported* assessments for Key Stage 1 in mathematics, science and English will be undertaken.

Academic year 1991/2

In the summer of 1992, the first *reported* assessments for Key Stage 1 in mathematics, science and English will take place. At the same time *unreported* assessments in mathematics and science for Key Stage 3 will be introduced.

Academic year 1992/3

In the autumn of 1992 attainment targets for Key Stage 4 (age group 15–16) will come into force for mathematics, science and English. During the summer of 1993 the first *reported* assessments for Key Stage 3 in mathematics and science will be mounted. At the same time, *unreported* assessments will be introduced for Key Stage 3 in English and technology, with a *reported* assessment for technology at Key Stage 1.

Academic year 1993/4

From the autumn of 1993, the attainment targets in technology for Key Stage 4 will become operative, and in the summer of 1994 *reported* assessments for Key Stage 3 in technology will take place.

At the same time, *unreported* assessments for Key Stage 2 in all the core subjects will be undertaken, along with *reported* assessments in English for Key Stage 3.

* for a description of the Key Stages see page 101

The attainment elements for GCSE (Key Stage 4) in mathematics, science and English will also be introduced in the summer of 1994.

Academic year 1994/5
In the summer of 1995 *reported* assessments will be undertaken for all the core subjects at Key Stage 2, and in technology for Key Stage 4.

FOUNDATION SUBJECTS

Academic year 1990/1
By the autumn of 1991 it is expected that for geography and history attainment targets and programmes of study will have been introduced for Key Stages 1, 2 and 3.

Academic year 1991/2
Autumn term 1992 is the provisional implementation date for attainment targets and programmes of study for modern languages, music, art and physical education at Key Stages 1, 2 and 3.

Academic year 1992/3
Standard attainment tests (SATs) for geography and history at Key Stage 1 are due to be introduced in the summer of 1993. These will be the first tests and will therefore be *unreported*.

Academic year 1993/4
Reported assessment for geography and history at Key Stage 1 will come into effect in the summer of 1994. At the same time *unreported* assessment for Key Stage 3 will take place. In the case of modern languages, music, art and physical education, *unreported* assessments at Key Stage 1 will become effective.
  In the autumn of 1994 Key Stage 4 in geography and history is provisionally planned to become operative.

Academic year 1994/5
Key Stage 2 with *unreported* assessment, and Key Stage 3 with *reported* assessment are due to be implemented for geography and history in the summer of 1995. At the same time, for modern languages, music, art and physical education, *reported* assessments will be introduced for Key Stage 1, along with *unreported* assessments for Key Stage 3.

Academic year 1995/6
Autumn 1995 will see the introduction of attainment targets and

programmes of study for Key Stage 4 in modern languages, music, art and physical education.

In summer 1996, *reported* assessments will be introduced for geography and history for Key Stage 2. At the same time, *unreported* GCSE/SAT reports become operative for Key Stage 4 in these subjects.

In the case of modern languages, music, art and physical education, *unreported* assessments will be due for Key Stage 2, and *reported* assessments for Key Stage 3.

Academic year 1996/7
In the summer of 1997, *reported* assessments will be due for modern languages, music, art and physical education at Key Stage 2, together with GCSE/SAT reports at Key Stage 4 (provisional).

Note: The modern languages timetable remains 'provisional'.

New nomenclature of classes and forms by age groupings

For National Curriculum standardisation of profiles and attainment test results it will be necessary to adopt a simple 'formula' which will identify the relevant age groups in schools.

For this purpose the key ages of 7, 11, 14 and 16 years will be the age of the majority of children in any given class or group and they will be identified by a year-group terminology as follows.

Reception classes (age five years or under)
Terminology: R

Infant classes (age five to seven years)
These will be known as years 1 and 2: nomenclature Yr1–2
(Key Stage 1)

Junior classes (age 7–11 years)
These classes will become years 3–6: nomenclature Yr3–6
(Key Stage 2)

Lower Secondary Classes (age 11–14 years)
These are to be termed years 7–9: nomenclature Yr7–9
(Key Stage 3)

Upper Secondary Classes (age 15–16 years)
These become years 10–11: nomenclature Yr10–11
(Key Stage 4)

Pupils aged 17 to 18 years will be classed as Yr12–13 but no key stages are specified for these years. Their new terminology officially replaces the traditional 'sixth formers' label.

Summary of the new curriculum framework

Before listing a summary of the draft Orders for the core subjects, it will be convenient to recapitulate the underlying curriculum framework:

1. *Attainment targets* (ATs)
   These are the sections or subdivisions of the National Curriculum subjects which, when taken together, comprise the total content of the subject study up to the age of 16+ years. These attainment targets vary in total from subject to subject. Thus the core subject of English is divided into five separate attainment targets. In the case of science there are no fewer than 17 separate attainment targets.

2. *Attainment levels*
   Each attainment target within each subject has a total of ten levels of attainment or achievement. Level 1 constitutes the first and easiest level and will be achieved in the early years of primary schooling. Level 10 constitutes the highest level of achievement. This will only be achieved by the brightest pupils and it requires a higher standard than that for GCSE at 16+ years.

3. *Programmes of study*
   Programmes of study are given alongside the draft Orders. They have no legal force and are presented in order to give examples of the type of school study which could lead to the achievement of the various attainment levels.

4. *The foundation subjects of the National Curriculum*
   These comprise the three core subjects of English, mathematics and science, taken together with the seven other foundation subjects which are history, modern languages, geography, art, physical education, music and technology.

Chapter 3

The National Curriculum in Practice and the Core Subjects

Summary of attainment targets for Levels 1–3: ENGLISH

ATTAINMENT TARGET 1: SPEAKING AND LISTENING

> The overall aim for Attainment Target 1 is described as:
>
> the development of pupils' understanding of the spoken word and the capacity to express themselves effectively in a variety of speaking and listening activities, matching style and response to audience and purpose.

Statements of attainment

Level 1 — Pupils should be able to:

(a) participate as speakers and listeners in group activities, including imaginative play;
(b) listen attentively, and respond, to stories and poems;
(c) respond appropriately to simple instructions given by a teacher.

Level 2 — Pupils should be able to:

(a) participate as speakers and listeners in a group engaged in a given task;
(b) describe an event, real or imagined, to the teacher or another pupil;
(c) listen attentively to stories and poems, and talk about them;
(d) talk with the teacher, listen, and ask and answer questions;
(e) respond appropriately to a range of more complex instructions given by a teacher, and give simple instructions.

Level 3 — Pupils should be able to:

(a) relate real or imaginary events in a connected narrative which conveys meaning to a group of pupils, the teacher or another known adult;
(b) convey accurately a simple message;
(c) listen with an increased span of concentration to other children and adults, asking and responding to questions and commenting on what has been said;
(d) give, receive and follow accurately, precise instructions when pursuing a task individually or as a member of a group.

ATTAINMENT TARGET 2: READING

The overall aim for Attainment Target 2 is described as:

the development of the ability to read, understand and respond to all types of writing, as well as the development of information-retrieval strategies for the purposes of study.

Statements of attainment
Level 1 — Pupils should:

(a) recognise that print is used to carry meaning, in books and in other forms in the everyday world;
(b) begin to recognise individual words or letters in familiar contexts;
(c) show signs of a developing interest in reading;
(d) talk in simple terms about the content of stories, or information in non-fiction books.

Level 2 — Pupils should be able to:

(a) read accurately and understand straightforward signs, labels and notices;
(b) demonstrate knowledge of the alphabet in using word books and simple dictionaries;
(c) use picture and context cues, words recognised on sight and phonic cues in reading;
(d) describe what has happened in a story and predict what may happen next;

(e) listen and respond to stories, poems and other material read aloud, expressing opinions informed by what has been read;

(f) read a range of material with some independence, fluency, accuracy and understanding.

Level 3 — Pupils should be able to:

(a) read aloud from familiar stories and poems fluently and with appropriate expression;

(b) read silently and with sustained concentration;

(c) listen attentively to stories, talk about setting, story-line and characters, and recall significant details;

(d) demonstrate, in talking about stories and poems, that they are beginning to use inference, deduction and previous reading experience to find and appreciate meanings beyond the literal;

(e) bring to their writing and discussion about stories some understanding of the way stories are structured;

(f) devise a clear set of questions that will enable them to select and use appropriate information sources and reference books from the class and school library.

ATTAINMENT TARGET 3: WRITING

The overall aim for Attainment Target 3 is described as:

A growing ability to construct and convey meaning in written language matching style to audience and purpose.

Statements of attainment
Level 1 — Pupils should be able to use pictures, symbols or isolated letters, words or phrases to communicate meaning.

Level 2 — Pupils should be able to:

(a) produce, independently, pieces of writing using complete sentences, some of them demarcated with capital letters and full stops or question marks;

(b) structure sequences of real or imagined events coherently in chronological accounts;

(c) write stories showing an understanding of the rudiments of story structure by establishing an opening, characters, and one or more events;

(d) produce simple, coherent non-chronological writing.

Level 3 — Pupils should be able to:

(a) produce, independently, pieces of writing using complete senten-ces, mainly demarcated with capital letters and full stops or question marks;
(b) shape chronological writing, beginning to use a wider range of sentence connectives than 'and' and 'then';
(c) write more complex stories with detail beyond simple events and with a defined ending;
(d) produce a range of types of non-chronological writing;
(e) begin to revise and redraft in discussion with the teacher, other adults or other children in the class, paying attention to meaning and clarity as well as checking for matters such as correct and consistent use of tenses and pronouns.

ATTAINMENT TARGET 4: SPELLING

Statements of attainment
Level 1 — Pupils should:

(a) begin to show an understanding of the difference between drawing and writing, and between numbers and letters;
(b) be able to write some letter shapes in response to speech sounds and letter names;
(c) be able to use at least single letters or groups of letters to represent whole words or parts of words.

Level 2 — Pupils should be able to:

(a) produce recognisable (though not necessarily always correct) spelling of a range of common words;
(b) spell correctly, in the course of their own writing, simple monosyllabic words they use regularly which observe common patterns;
(c) recognise that spelling has patterns, and begin to apply their knowledge of those patterns in their attempts to spell a wider range of words;
(d) show knowledge of the names and order of the letters of the alphabet.

Level 3 — Pupils should be able to:

(a) spell correctly, in the course of their own writing, simple polysyllabic words they use regularly which observe common patterns;
(b) recognise and use correctly regular patterns for vowel sounds and common letter strings;
(c) show a growing awareness of word families and their relationships;
(d) in revising and redrafting their writing, begin to check the accuracy of their spelling.

ATTAINMENT TARGET 5: HANDWRITING

Statements of attainment
Level 1 — Pupils should begin to form letters with some control over the size, shape and orientation of letters or lines of writing.

Level 2 — Pupils should be able to:

(a) produce legible upper and lower case letters in one style and use them consistently (ie not randomly mixed within words);
(b) produce letters that are recognisably formed and properly oriented and that have clear ascenders and descenders where necessary;

Level 3 — Pupils should begin to produce clear and legible joined-up writing.

Summary of attainment targets for Levels 1–3: SCIENCE

ATTAINMENT TARGET 1: EXPLORATION OF SCIENCE

The overall aim for Attainment Target 1 is described as:

Pupils should develop the intellectual and practical skills that allow them to explore the world of science and to develop a fuller understanding of scientific phenomena and the procedures of scientific exploration and investigation. This work should take place in the context of activities that require a progressively more systematic and quantified approach, which draws upon an increasing knowledge and understanding of science.

Statements of attainment
Level 1 — Pupils should be able to:

(a) observe familiar materials and events in their immediate environment, at first hand, using their senses;
(b) describe and communicate their observations, ideally through talking in groups or by other means, within their class.

Level 2 — Pupils should be able to:

(a) ask questions and suggest ideas of the 'how', 'why', and 'what will happen if' variety;
(b) identify simple differences, for example, hot/cold, rough/smooth;
(c) use non-standard and standard measures, for example, hand-spans and rulers;
(d) list and collate observations;
(e) interpret findings by associating one factor with another;
(f) record findings in charts, drawings and other appropriate forms.

Level 3 — Pupils should be able to:

(a) formulate hypotheses;
(b) identify and describe simple variables that change over time;
(c) distinguish between a 'fair' and an 'unfair' test;
(d) select and use simple instruments to enhance observation;
(e) quantify variables, as appropriate, to the nearest labelled division of simple measuring instruments;
(f) record experimental findings;
(g) interpret simple pictograms and bar charts;
(h) interpret observations in terms of a generalised statement;
(i) describe activities carried out by sequencing the major features.

ATTAINMENT TARGET 2: THE VARIETY OF LIFE

The overall aim for Attainment Target 2 is described as:

Pupils should develop their knowledge and understanding of the diversity and classification of past and present life-forms, and of the relationships, energy flows, cycles of matter and human influences within ecosystems.

Statements of attainment
Level 1 — Pupils should know that there is a wide variety of living things, which includes human beings.

Level 2 — Pupils should:

(a) know that plants and animals need certain conditions to sustain life;
(b) understand how living things are looked after and be able to treat them with care and consideration.

Level 3 — Pupils should:

(a) recognise similarities and differences among living things;
(b) sort living things into broad groups according to observable features;
(c) know that living things respond to seasonal and daily changes.

ATTAINMENT TARGET 3: PROCESSES OF LIFE

The overall aim for Attainment Target 3 is described as:

Pupils should develop their knowledge and understanding of the organisation of living things and of the processes which characterise their survival and reproduction.

Statements of attainment
Level 1 — Pupils should be able to name or label the external parts of the human body/plants.

Level 2 — Pupils should:

(a) know that living things reproduce their own kind;
(b) know that personal hygiene, food, exercise, rest and safety, and the proper and safe use of medicines are important;
(c) be able to give a simple account of the pattern of their own day.

Level 3 — Pupils should:

(a) know that the basic life processes — feeding, breathing,

movement and behaviour — are common to human beings and
the other living things they have studied;

(b) be able to describe the main stages in the human life cycle.

ATTAINMENT TARGET 4: GENETICS AND EVOLUTION

The overall aim for Attainment Target 4 is described as:

Pupils should develop their knowledge and understanding of variation
and its genetic and environmental causes and the basic mechanisms of
inheritance, selection and evolution.

Statements of attainment

Level 1 — Pupils should know that human beings vary from one
individual to the next.

Level 2 — Pupils should be able to measure simple differences between
each other.

Level 3 — Pupils should know that some life forms became extinct a
long time ago and others more recently.

ATTAINMENT TARGET 5: HUMAN INFLUENCES ON THE EARTH

The overall aim for Attainment Target 5 is described as:

Pupils should develop knowledge and understanding of the ways in
which human activities affect the Earth.

Statements of attainment

Level 1 — Pupils should know that human activities produce a wide
range of waste products.

Level 2 — Pupils should:

(a) know that some waste products decay naturally but often do so
over a long period of time;
(b) be able to keep a diary, in a variety of forms, of change over time.

Level 3 — Pupils should:

(a) know that human activity may produce local changes in the Earth's surface, air and water;
(b) be able to give an account of a project to help improve the local environment.

ATTAINMENT TARGET 6: TYPES AND USES OF MATERIALS

The overall aim for Attainment Target 6 is described as:

Pupils should develop their knowledge and understanding of the properties of materials and the way properties of materials determine their uses and form the basis for their classification.

Statements of attainment
Level 1 — Pupils should be able to describe familiar and unfamiliar objects in terms of simple properties.

Level 2 — Pupils should:

(a) be able to recognise important similarities and differences, including hardness, flexibility and transparency, in the characteristics of materials;
(b) be able to group materials according to their characteristics;
(c) know that heating and cooling materials can cause them to melt, solidify or change permanently.

Level 3 — Pupils should:

(a) know that some materials occur naturally while many are made from raw materials;
(b) be able to list the similarities and differences in a variety of everyday materials.

ATTAINMENT TARGET 7: MAKING NEW MATERIALS

The overall aim for Attainment Target 7 is described as:

Pupils should develop their knowledge and understanding of the process of changing materials by chemical reaction and the way this is used in the manufacture of new materials.

Statements of attainment

No statutory order for Levels 1–3 has been laid for Attainment Target 7.

ATTAINMENT TARGET 8: EXPLAINING HOW MATERIALS BEHAVE

The overall aim for Attainment Target 8 is described as:

Pupils should develop their knowledge and understanding of the use of models to explain the structure and properties of materials.

Statements of attainment

No statutory order for Levels 1–3 has been laid for Attainment Target 8.

ATTAINMENT TARGET 9: EARTH AND ATMOSPHERE

The overall aim for Attainment Target 9 is described as:

Pupils should develop their knowledge and understanding of the structure and main features of the Earth, the atmosphere and their changes over time.

Statements of attainment

Level 1 — Pupils should:

(a) know that there is a variety of weather conditions;
(b) be able to describe changes in the weather.

Level 2 — Pupils should:

(a) know that there are patterns in the weather which are related to seasonal changes;
(b) know that the weather has a powerful effect on people's lives;
(c) be able to record the weather over a period to time, in words, drawings and charts or other forms of communication;
(d) be able to sort natural materials into broad groups according to observable features.

Level 3 — Pupils should:

(a) be able to describe from their observations some of the effects of weathering on buildings and on the landscape;
(b) know that air is all around us;
(c) understand how weathering of rocks leads to the formation of different types of soil;
(d) be able to give an account of an investigation of some natural material (rock or soil);
(e) be able to understand and interpret common meteorological symbols as used in the media.

ATTAINMENT TARGET 10: FORCES

The overall aim for Attainment Target 10 is described as:

Pupils should develop their knowledge and understanding of forces; their nature, significance and effects on the movement of objects.

Statements of Attainment
Level 1 — Pupils should know that things can be moved by pushing them.

Level 2 — Pupils should understand that pushes and pulls can make things start moving, speed up, swerve or stop.

Level 3 — Pupils should:

(a) understand that when things are changed in shape, begin to move or stop moving, forces are acting on them;
(b) understand the factors which cause objects to float or sink in water.

ATTAINMENT TARGET 11: ELECTRICITY AND MAGNETISM

The overall aim for Attainment Target 11 is described as:

Pupils should develop their knowledge and understanding of electric and electromagnetic effects in simple circuits, electric devices and domestic appliances.

Statements of attainment
Level 1 — Pupils should know that many household appliances use electricity but that misuse could be dangerous.

Level 2 — Pupils should:

(a) know that magnets attract certain materials but not others and can repel each other;
(b) understand the danger associated with the use of electricity and know appropriate safety measures.

Level 3 — Pupils should:

(a) know that some materials conduct electricity well while others do not;
(b) understand that a complete circuit is needed for an electrical device, such as a bulb or buzzer, to work.

ATTAINMENT TARGET 12: THE SCIENTIFIC ASPECTS OF INFORMATION TECHNOLOGY INCLUDING MICROELECTRONICS

The overall aim for Attainment Target 12 is described as:

Pupils should develop their knowledge and understanding of information transfer and microelectronics.

Statements of attainment
Level 1 — Pupils should know about some everyday devices which receive text, sound and image over long distances, using information technology.

Level 2 — Pupils should:

(a) know that there is a variety of means for communication over long distances;
(b) know that information can be stored using a range of everyday devices, including the computer.

Level 3 — Pupils should:

(a) be able to store information using devices;
(b) know that information can be stored electronically in a variety of ways;
(c) be able to retrieve and select text, number, sound or graphics stored on a computer.

ATTAINMENT TARGET 13: ENERGY

The overall aim for Attainment Target 13 is described as:

Pupils should develop their knowledge and understanding of the nature of energy, its transfer and control. They should develop their knowledge and understanding of the range of energy sources and the issues involved in their exploitation.

Statements of attainment
Level 1 — Pupils should:

(a) understand that they need food to be active;
(b) be able to describe, by talking or other appropriate means, how food is necessary for life.

Level 2 — Pupils should:

(a) understand the meaning of 'hot' and 'cold' relative to the temperature of their own bodies;
(b) be able to describe how a toy with a simple mechanism which moves and stores energy works.

Level 3 — Pupils should:

(a) understand, in qualitative terms, that models and machines need a source of energy in order to work;
(b) know that temperature is a measure of how hot (or cold) things are;
(c) be able to use simple power sources (electric motors, rubber bands) and devices which transfer energy (gears, belts, levers).

ATTAINMENT TARGET 14: SOUND AND MUSIC

> The overall aim for Attainment Target 14 is described as:
>
> Pupils should develop their knowledge and understanding of the properties, transmission and absorption of sound.

Statements of attainment
Level 1 — Pupils should know that sounds can be made in a variety of ways.

Level 2 — Pupils should:

(a) know that sounds are heard when the sound reaches the ear;
(b) be able to explain how musical sounds are produced in simple musical instruments.

Level 3 — Pupils should:

(a) know that sounds are produced by vibrating objects and can travel through different materials;
(b) be able to give a simple explanation of the way in which sound is generated and can travel through different materials.

ATTAINMENT TARGET 15: USING LIGHT AND ELECTROMAGNETIC RADIATION

> The overall aim for Attainment Target 15 is described as:
>
> Pupils should develop their knowledge and understanding of the properties and behaviour of light and electromagnetic waves.

Statements of attainment
Level 1 — Pupils should:

(a) know that light comes from different sources;
(b) be able to discriminate between colours and match them or, where appropriate, demonstrate an understanding of colour in the environment.

Level 2 — Pupils should:

(a) know that light passes through some materials and not others, and that when it does not, shadows may be formed;
(b) be able to draw pictures, showing features such as light, colour and shade.

Level 3 — Pupils should:

(a) know that light can be made to change direction and shiny surfaces can form images;
(b) be able to give an account of an investigation with mirrors.

ATTAINMENT TARGET 16: THE EARTH IN SPACE

> The overall aim for Attainment Target 16 is described as:
>
> Pupils should develop their knowledge and understanding of the relative positions and movement of the Earth, moon, sun and solar system within the universe.

Statements of attainment
Level 1 — Pupils should:

(a) be able to describe through talking, or other appropriate means, the seasonal changes that occur in the weather and in living things;
(b) know the danger of looking directly at the sun;
(c) be able to describe, in relation to their home or school, the apparent daily motion of the sun across the sky.

Level 2

(a) be able to explain why night occurs;
(b) know that day length changes throughout the year;
(c) know that we live on a large, spherical, self-contained planet called Earth;
(d) know that the Earth, moon and sun are separate bodies.

Level 3

   (a) know that the inclination of the sun in the sky changes during the year;
   (b) be able to measure time with a sundial.

ATTAINMENT TARGET 17: THE NATURE OF SCIENCE

The overall aim for Attainment Target 17 is described as:

Pupils should develop their knowledge and understanding of the way in which scientific ideas change through time and how the nature of these ideas and the uses to which they are put are affected by the social, moral, spiritual and cultural contexts in which they are developed; in doing so, they should begin to recognise that while science is an important way of thinking about experience, it is not the only way.

Statements of attainment
No statutory order for Levels 1–3 has been laid for Attainment Target 17.

Summary of attainment targets for Levels 1–3: MATHEMATICS

ATTAINMENT TARGET 1: USING AND APPLYING MATHEMATICS

The overall aim for Attainment Target 1 is described as:

Pupils should use number, algebra and measures in practical tasks, in real-life problems, and to investigate within mathematics itself.

Statements of attainment
Level 1 — Pupils should:

   (a) use materials provided for a task;
   (b) talk about their own work and ask questions;
   (c) make predictions based on experience.

Level 2 — Pupils should:

(a) select the materials and the mathematics to use for a task;
(b) describe current work, record findings and check results;
(c) ask and respond to the question: 'What would happen if …?'

Level 3 — Pupils should:

(a) select the materials and the mathematics to use for a task; check results and consider whether they are sensible;
(b) explain work being done and record findings systematically;
(c) make and test predictions.

ATTAINMENT TARGET 2: NUMBER

Statements of attainment
Level 1 — Pupils should be able to:

(a) count, read, write and order numbers to at least ten, know that the size of a set is given by the last number in the count;
(b) understand the conservation of number.

Level 2 — Pupils should be able to:

(a) read, write and order numbers to at least 100, use the knowledge that the tens-digit indicates the number of tens;
(b) understand the meaning of 'a half' and 'a quarter'.

Level 3 — Pupils should be able to:

(a) read, write and order numbers to at least 1,000, use the knowledge that the position of a digit indicates its value;
(b) use decimal notation as the conventional way of recording in money;
(c) appreciate the meaning of negative whole numbers in familiar contexts.

ATTAINMENT TARGET 3: NUMBER

> The overall aim of Attainment Target 3 is described as:
>
> Pupils should understand number operations (addition, subtraction, multiplication and division) and make use of appropriate methods of calculation.

Statements of attainment

Level 1 — Pupils should be able to add or subtract, using objects where the numbers involved are not greater than ten.

Level 2 — Pupils should:

- (a) know and use addition and subtraction facts up to ten.
- (b) be able to compare two numbers to find the difference;
- (c) be able to solve whole number problems involving addition and subtraction, including money.

Level 3 — Pupils should:

- (a) know and use addition and subtraction number facts to 20 (including zero);
- (b) be able to solve problems involving multiplication or division of whole numbers or money, using a calculator where necessary;
- (c) know and use multiplication facts up to five x five, and all those in twice, five and ten times multiplication tables.

ATTAINMENT TARGET 4: NUMBER

> The overall aim of Attainment Target 4 is described as:
>
> Pupils should estimate and approximate in number.

Statements of attainment

Level 1 — Pupils should be able to give a sensible estimate of a small number of objects (up to ten).

Level 2 — Pupils should be able to make a sensible estimate of a number of objects up to 20.

Level 3 — Pupils should:

(a) recognise that the first digit is the most important in indicating the size of a number, and approximate to the nearest 10 or 100;
(b) understand 'remainders' given the context of calculation, and know whether to round up or down.

ATTAINMENT TARGET 5: NUMBER/ALGEBRA

> The overall aim of Attainment Target 5 is described as:
>
> Pupils should recognise and use patterns, relationships and sequences and make generalisations.

Statements of attainment
Level 1 — Pupils should be able to copy, continue and devise repeating patterns represented by objects/apparatus or one-digit numbers.

Level 2 — Pupils should be able to:

(a) explore and use the patterns in addition and subtraction facts to ten;
(b) distinguish between odd and even numbers.

Level 3 — Pupils should be able to:

(a) explain number patterns and predict subsequent numbers where appropriate;
(b) find number patterns and equivalent forms of two-digit numbers and use these to perform mental calculations;
(c) recognise whole numbers which are exactly divisible by two, five and ten.

ATTAINMENT TARGET 6: ALGEBRA

> The overall aim of Attainment Target 6 is described as:
>
> Pupils should recognise and use functions, formulae, equations and inequalities.

Statements of attainment

Level 2 — Pupils should understand the use of a symbol to stand for an unknown number.

Level 3 — Pupils should be able to deal with inputs to and outputs from simple function machines.

Note: No statutory order has been laid for Level 1 of Attainment Target 6.

ATTAINMENT TARGET 7: ALGEBRA

> The overall aim of Attainment Target 7 is described as:
>
> Pupils should use graphical representation of algebraic functions.

Statements of attainment

No statutory order for Levels 1–3 has been laid for Attainment Target 7.

ATTAINMENT TARGET 8: MEASURES

> The overall aim of Attainment Target 8 is described as:
>
> Pupils should estimate and measure quantities, and appreciate the approximate nature of measurement.

Statements of attainment

Level 1 — Pupils should be able to compare and order objects without measuring, and use appropriate language.

Level 2 — Pupils should:

(a) be able to use non-standard measures in length, area, volume, capacity, 'weight' and time to compare objects and recognise the need to use standard units;
(b) know how to use coins in simple contexts;
(c) know the most commonly used units in length, capacity, 'weight' and time, and what they are used for.

Level 3 — Pupils should be able to:

(a) use a wider range of metric units;
(b) choose and use appropriate units and instruments in a variety of situations, interpreting numbers on a range of measuring instruments;
(c) make estimates based on familiar units.

ATTAINMENT TARGET 9: USING AND APPLYING MATHEMATICS

The overall aim of Attainment Target 9 is described as:

Pupils should use shape and space and handle data in practical tasks, in real-life problems, and to investigate within mathematics itself.

Statements of attainment
Level 1 — Pupils should be able to:

(a) use materials provided for a task;
(b) talk about their own work and ask questions;
(c) make predictions based on experience.

Level 2 — Pupils should be able to:

(a) select the materials and the mathematics to use for a task;
(b) describe current work, record findings and check results;
(c) ask and respond to the question: 'What would happen if …?'

Level 3 — Pupils should be able to:

(a) select the materials and the mathematics to use for a task — check results and consider whether they are sensible;
(b) explain work being done and record findings systematically;
(c) make and test predictions.

ATTAINMENT TARGET 10: SHAPE AND SPACE

The overall aim of Attainment Target 10 is described as:

Pupils should recognise and use the properties of two-dimensional and three-dimensional shapes.

Statements of attainment
Level 1 — Pupils should be able to:

   (a) sort 3-D and 2-D shapes;
   (b) build with 3-D solid shapes and draw 2-D shapes and describe them.

Level 2 — Pupils should be able to:

   (a) recognise squares, rectangles, circles, triangles, hexagons, pentagons, cubes, rectangular boxes (cuboids), cylinders and spheres, and describe them;
   (b) recognise right-angled corners in 2-D and 3-D shapes.

Level 3 — Pupils should be able to sort 2-D and 3-D shapes in different ways and give reasons for each method of sorting.

ATTAINMENT TARGET 11: SHAPE AND SPACE

> The overall aim of Attainment Target 11 is described as:
>
> Pupils should recognise location and use transformations in the study of space.

Statements of attainment
Level 1 — Pupils should be able to:

   (a) state a position using prepositions such as: on, inside, above, under, behind, next to etc;
   (b) give and understand instructions for moving along a line.

Level 2 — Pupils should be able to:

   (a) understand the notion of angle;
   (b) give and understand instructions for turning through right-angles;
   (c) recognise different types of movement: straight movement (translation); turning movement (rotation); flip movement (reflection).

Level 3 — Pupils should be able to:

(a) recognise the (reflective) symmetry in a variety of shapes in 2 and 3 dimensions;
(b) understand eight points of the compass; use clockwise and anti-clockwise appropriately.

ATTAINMENT TARGET 12: HANDLING DATA

The overall aim of Attainment Target 12 is described as:

Pupils should collect, record and process data.

Statements of attainment
Level 1 — Pupils should be able to select criteria for sorting a set of objects and apply them consistently.

Level 2 — Pupils should be able to:

(a) choose criteria to sort and classify objects; record the results of observations or outcomes of events;
(b) help to design a data collection sheet and use it to record a set of data leading to a frequency table.

Level 3 — Pupils should be able to:

(a) extract specific pieces of information from tables and lists;
(b) enter and access information in a simple database.

ATTAINMENT TARGET 13: HANDLING DATA

The overall aim of Attainment Target 13 is described as:

Pupils should represent and interpret data.

Statements of attainment
Level 1 — Pupils should be able to:

(a) record with real objects or drawings and comment about the result;

(b) create simple mapping diagrams showing relationships, and to read and interpret them.

Level 2 — Pupils should be able to construct, read and interpret block graphs and frequency tables.

Level 3 — Pupils should be able to:

(a) construct and interpret bar charts;
(b) create and interpret graphs (pictograms) where the symbol represents a group of units.

ATTAINMENT TARGET 14: HANDLING DATA

The overall aim of Attainment Target 14 is described as:

Pupils should understand, estimate and calculate probabilities.

Statements of attainment
Level 1 — Pupils should be able to recognise possible outcomes of simple random events.

Level 2 — Pupils should be able to recognise that there is a degree of uncertainty about the outcome of some events and other events are certain or impossible.

Level 3 — Pupils should be able to:

(a) place events in order of 'likelihood' and use appropriate words to identify the chance;
(b) understand and use the idea of 'events' and say whether events are more or less likely than this;
(c) distinguish between 'fair' and 'unfair'.

Chapter 4

Educational Management and the National Curriculum

The major changes in the educational framework which the introduction of the National Curriculum demanded could neither be conceived nor executed in a vacuum. Of necessity, they had to be grafted into an existing system where many other major factors were already at work. Thus the following factors will strongly influence the success of the National Curriculum proposals:

1. teacher supply and quality;
2. school buildings;
3. local management of schools;
4. opting out;
5. continuity of schooling;
6. school organisational styles.

Teacher supply

By the turn of the decade demographic factors were becoming increasingly ominous and in an effort to head off impending teacher shortages of major proportions, the DES initiated the following changes in the concept of teacher probation and in the long-standing arrangements for reaching qualified teacher status.

1. *Probationary year arrangements*
   From late 1989 existing 'probationary year arrangements' whereby a teacher's status in a maintained schools system was confirmed, subject to satisfactory performance, after the first year of teaching, were modified. In support of this proposal the Secretary of State made the point that fewer than ten teachers per year failed to complete their probationary year successfully. Additionally it was

declared that probationary teacher arrangements were both cum-
bersome and difficult to operate.

2. *Qualified teacher status and licensed teachers*
   Prior to 1989, in addition to the normal teacher training route
   leading to qualified teacher status, there existed a number of what
   were termed 'non-standard routes'. From autumn 1989 all these
   non-standard routes were abolished and were replaced by a single
   non-standard route. The award of qualified teacher status for
   students choosing the new non-standard route would depend upon
   the recommendation of an employer (usually the LEA). This award
   on the non-standard route would be achieved in two stages.

   (i) In the *first stage* the employer would recommend that the
   person be granted a 'licence to teach'.
   (ii) In the *second stage*, the licensed teacher would become eligible,
   after two years, for qualified teacher status based upon the
   recommendation of the employer. During the licensed teacher
   period, the candidate is required to undertake such training as
   the employer deems appropriate. (This could involve a programme in conjunction with a neighbouring teacher training
   institution.)
   (iii) At the end of the licensed teacher period the Secretary of State
   would grant qualified teacher status in the light of the
   employer's recommendation.
   (iv) All licensees must have the equivalent of two years of higher
   education in the UK in addition to the equivalent of a grade 'C'
   in GCSE mathematics and English. Furthermore, the minimum age for entry will be 26.

GRADUATE TWO-YEAR ON-THE-JOB TRAINING
In addition to the 'licensed teacher' scheme the Secretary of State
proposed that LEAs and teacher training institutions should devise
experimental schemes of school-based training over a two-year period,
for recent graduates and mature entrants. These schemes were
crystallised into what has come to be known as the *articled teacher*
route to qualified teacher status. The articled teacher route commenced
in September 1989 with a provision for up to 600 graduates to be
enrolled in the scheme.

CHANGES IN INITIAL TEACHER TRAINING
As far as initial teacher training was concerned, the introduction of the
National Curriculum resulted in the issue of a DES consultative

document which proposed a reconstitution of the Council for the Accreditation of Teacher Education (CATE).

Under the new proposals, CATE would advise on course accreditation and the powers of the local committees to monitor and vet existing courses in teacher education would be strengthened.

Additionally, the DES announced new criteria for initial teacher training courses.

Thus colleges will be required to:

1. Set out in detail the knowledge and skills which they expect the students to acquire.
2. Take full account of the needs of the National Curriculum.
3. Ensure that primary training students spend 100 hours on science as well as 100 hours on mathematics and English.
4. Ensure that teacher training lecturers spend a term every five years in a school (from 1992).
5. Continue the requirement that all primary teacher training students must study the teaching of religious education.

STAFFING NEEDS FOR THE NATIONAL CURRICULUM

The Association of Metropolitan Authorities estimated that the needs of the National Curriculum would require an additional 6,000 teachers from 1989 onwards, with the prospect of a further 60,000 teachers required by the year 2000.

In the specialist subject fields, estimates of teacher shortages in mathematics have been estimated in the region of 4,000 by the year 1995 (assuming that the present rate of recruitment is maintained). Similarly in the field of modern languages the implications of the foundation subject requirements could require the recruitment of an additional 3,000 teachers by the time that the assessment and testing arrangements at secondary level are fully operative.

DES FINANCIAL ALLOCATIONS 1989/90 AND 1990/91

For the 1989/90 financial year the DES increased the total of £207 million to £214 million, with the addition of approximately £80 million from the LEAs. It was reckoned that the total amount available for the in-service training of teachers would approach £300 million, with a further increase to £325 million for 1990/91.

Of this total of £300 million, over £80 million was earmarked for expenditure on training in national priority areas concerning the introduction of the National Curriculum.

On the LEA side it was notable that the allocation for training for the

National Curriculum in the areas of management and assessment was increased from £17 million to £33.1 million. Similarly provision for training for the National Curriculum content was increased from £41 million to £48.8 million.

Teacher quality

The introduction of the BEd degree course at honours level for intending teachers, combined with tighter regulation of the content of both first degree and PGCE teacher training courses, has led to a marked improvement in the standard of competence of entrants to the profession over recent years.

The demands of the National Curriculum will nevertheless stretch the competences of teachers to the utmost. A teaching body which is adequately rewarded in terms of status and remuneration may be expected to exhibit a number of essential professional qualities which will assist them to deal confidently with the challenges which are now presenting themselves.

Thus good teachers should:

1. Be prepared to keep up to date by means of in-service courses, membership of professional groups, and the interchange of ideas and practices between schools.
2. Adopt a relaxed and calm manner in the classroom, be aware of each child as an individual, and exhibit a sense of enthusiasm and purpose in their work.
3. Adopt varied patterns of working and use differing approaches to their lessons.
4. Appreciate fully the abilities of their pupils and raise expectations as high as possible.
5. Organise their teaching programme in a logical and progressive way and be aware of the need for management and leadership skills.
6. Assess and record the progress of individual children carefully and explicitly.
7. Contribute to the overall climate or 'ethos' of the school.
8. Maintain a good example for their pupils through their own personal standards.
9. Foster opportunities for parental and community awareness and participation in the life and work of the school.

Buildings and resources

The implementation of the National Curriculum is taking place at a time when the backlog of maintenance and improvement to school premises, especially at secondary level, has been exceptionally severe. As a result, many schools have *premises* which can only be described as dilapidated and urgently in need of redecoration, repair and additional maintenance. Over the last few years the picture appears to have continued to deteriorate. Furthermore, the supply of *books*, *equipment* and *materials* in schools varies considerably and, in particular, school library provision and staffing have been subject to neglect and inadequacy in many of them.

Remedying these deficiencies from the past will require extensive capital and initial grant expenditure, but this is essential if the National Curriculum is to develop in an atmosphere which is cheerful, well resourced and balanced in terms of quality and purpose.

Local management of schools

From 1990 most maintained schools will be operating devolved financial management systems, commonly known as 'local management of schools' (LMS).

Under this system, schools, according to schemes approved by the DES, will be responsible for the major share of the financial budget formerly managed by the LEAs. Although LMS will provide much more freedom for individual schools to manage their financial affairs, school governors will be faced with invidious choices which were previously shouldered by the LEA. Full accountability must be observed and many schools may be faced with financial responsibilities which leave them with less room for manoeuvre than they previously had. Thus surveys indicate that four out of ten primary schools and six out of ten secondary schools will be 'worse off' under devolved financial management.

Financial control problems will hit smaller schools particularly severely and cannot but be a disincentive to the implementation of the National Curriculum.

Opting out

The number of schools 'opting out' and receiving grant-maintained status is increasing. These schools will be funded directly by the DES and although they are physically located within the boundaries of an LEA, they will no longer be funded by that LEA.

Grant-maintained schools, as distinct from independent schools, are obliged to implement the National Curriculum. They will, however, lack the back-up which maintained schools receive from the LEA. Thus parts of existing library stock may be removed by the LEA and grant-maintained schools will not have an automatic right to the use of shared facilities such as playing fields, swimming baths etc.

Furthermore, they will not benefit from the economies of scale, and the pooled advice and help, especially on National Curriculum questions, which will be available to maintained schools via the LEA advisory services and county National Curriculum planning arrangements.

Continuity of schooling

As children move to different schools at the traditional 'age breaks' of 7 and 11 years, care has always needed to be taken to ensure that they feel at home in their new school, that they are properly prepared for the move, that parents are kept fully in touch about the transfers and that continuity of curricular progress is well recorded and maintained. These considerations apply with equal force to situations where transfer occurs at a 'middle school' stage of 8 or 9 years, and when the secondary stage commences at 12 or 13 years.

The demands made by the implementation of the National Curriculum, with its key stage assessment implications, will necessitate a strengthening of existing transfer continuity arrangements, with careful attention being paid to a number of major points.

ADMINISTRATION

1. Transfer arrangements need to be published in a clearly understood form and distributed to the parents and teachers of both the primary and secondary or middle schools concerned.

2. Record cards of individual pupils need to be available to the receiving school, and in addition to standard subject performance information they should provide material covering the full age range of the pupil's abilities, interests and achivements, together with a statement of his or her 'pastoral' needs.

3. Information about the 'friendship grouping' of the primary school should be provided.

4. Visits to the receiving school should be undertaken well before the time of transfer: a real introduction to the new stage of schooling

could be provided through arranging specimen lessons and activities for the newcomers during the summer term.

CURRICULUM MANAGEMENT
Curriculum continuity demands well-planned liaison between individual schools, or groups of schools, and it needs to be supported by teachers' centre and in-service arrangements which can focus upon this particular topic.

Interesting examples of school liaison were given in *Education Observed (10): Curriculum Continuity at 11+* (DES, 1989). In one example, children in their final term at primary school had periods of practical instruction in subjects which were not available in their own school, such as cricket and hockey. At the same time they were introduced to specialist provision in the shape of science laboratories and home economics and craft rooms.

A further example of good practice occurred when teachers at the primary and secondary schools 'changed places' for short periods of time. This arrangement was particularly helpful when consultative groups had planned the continuation at secondary school level of a topic which had been started in the primary school.

As already noted, the question of curriculum continuity needs particular emphasis where transfer between schools occurs at varying ages, notably in middle school arrangements.

At whatever age transfer of schooling takes place there are hopes as well as fears for its influence upon the implementation of the National Curriculum. Thus, on an optimistic note, it was commented in *From Policy to Practice* (DES, 1988) that in all schools and for all teachers:

> the National Curriculum will not only represent a new framework for individual and school activity, but will also enable that activity to be related to what is going on in other schools and classrooms. Teachers can have greater confidence that they are making the best possible contribution to pupils' needs over time and across the range of subjects; and will have a sounder basis for dialogue between schools and with colleagues. The moderation arrangements will provide a focus for this kind of exchange of views and experience.

School organisational styles

Although the National Curriculum lays down attainment targets and specifies key stages for assessment and testing, the Education Reform Act itself excluded any reference to time allocations, teaching methods and internal school organisation.

In practical situations, however, schools will be faced with problems such as:

1. How can a small primary school cover all the foundation subject areas specified in the National Curriculum?
2. How can the subject teaching indicated in the individual attainment targets be reconciled with the integrated topic approach commonly adopted for the 5–11 age range?
3. How much time will be left for learning situations which do not lie within the National Curriculum core and foundation frameworks?
4. What will be the effect of transfer of children from or to the independent school system, or in connection with HM Forces postings from abroad?
5. Although the key stages correspond with school transfer and leaving dates in many counties, how will the middle school transfer system be effected, where moves may occur at 8, 12 or 13 years of age?

MANAGEMENT CONSIDERATIONS AT SCHOOL LEVEL
National Curriculum requirements have important consequences for the internal management of schools. Thus:

1. A whole school approach to the curriculum, with detailed planning and management, is vital.
2. Existing structures need rethinking to allow for flexibility, continuity and an inter-school approach.
3. A study of the whole range of available resources is necessary.

Put in terms of management objectives, the following questions arise:

1. What will be the best form of grouping of pupils in the light of the requirements of the National Curriculum.
2. Should staff continue to operate in 'traditional' classteacher roles: is this the best way to deploy increasingly scarce human teaching resources?
3. How can a school's schemes of work integrate the National Curriculum attainment needs into an approach which covers the whole school curriculum?
4. What steps will need to be taken to secure the effective monitoring of the progress of each child?

5. How can it be ensured that flows of information and communication networks at school, LEA and DES level are adequate?
6. What steps need to be taken to keep parents fully informed of the implications of the National Curriculum?
7. How can school governors best be brought to play their full part in the curriculum process? (Especially in view of the fact that the governors are responsible to the Secretary of State for the implementation of the National Curriculum in their school.)

Chapter 5

Curriculum Issues

Religious education and the National Curriculum

Religious education was not specified in the 1988 Education Reform Act as one of the foundation subjects. However, it was remarked that it constituted an essential part of the work and life of all maintained schools and sixth form colleges. The requirements do not however apply to tertiary colleges, FE colleges or nursery schools or classes.

The 1988 Act reinforced the arrangements originally laid down in the 1944 Butler Act for *acts of collective worship* and for religious education as part of the school curriculum. Thus it was stated that the curriculum should:

> promote the spiritual, moral, cultural, mental and physical development of pupils at the school and of society; and prepare such pupils for the opportunities, responsibilities and experiences of adult life.

It was also stressed that the responsibility for religious education should include respect, understanding and tolerance for people who hold different faiths.

The 1988 Education Reform Act reinforced the 1944 stipulation that there must be religious education provision for *all pupils*. Furthermore, it was reasserted that:

1. Religious education in county schools must be non-denominational and be in accordance with a locally agreed syllabus.
2. The parental right of withdrawal which was included in the 1944 Act is retained.
3. The safeguards for teachers who do not wish to participate remain unchanged.

Nevertheless, the 1988 Act introduced some important new elements into the framework of religious education teaching:

1. New local syllabuses must take into account the religious tradition of the country, which is mainly Christian. At the same time, note must be taken of the teaching and practice of other principal religions.
2. Although religious education must not be denominational in county schools, there is no objection to lessons which highlight the differences between denominations.
3. Standing Advisory Councils on Religious Education (SACRE) *must* be set up, with a specification composition. The functions of the SACRE are to be extended.
4. The SACRE is empowered to require an LEA to arrange a conference to review the agreed syllabus.

The 1944 Education Act provisions for collective worship were not changed in the 1988 Act. Thus:

1. There must be a daily act of collective worship for all pupils: in county schools this must be non-denominational.
2. The parental rights of withdrawal and the safeguards for teachers remain.

However, the 1988 Act did introduce the following amendments to the 1944 Act requirements:

1. The daily act of collective worship may now be arranged for *separate* groups of pupils.
2. The act of worship may now take place at any time during the school day.
3. The act of worship must be of a wholly or mainly Christian character.
4. The act of worship must not be distinctive of any particular Christian denomination.

In cases where the requirements *cannot be met*, either for the whole school or for a particular group of pupils, the headteacher is empowered to apply to the SACRE, with the purpose of securing a ruling that the requirements for Christian collective worship should not apply.

Following the 1988 Act, religious education is considered to be part of the *basic* curriculum of schools. Religious education does not figure as one of the core or other foundation subjects but nevertheless a conference may propose a locally determined religious education syllabus which can include attainment targets, programmes of study and assessment arrangements.

The situation was summed up in paragraph 20 of the Department of Education and Science Circular 3/89, *The Education Reform Act 1988: Religious Education and Collective Worship*:

> The special status of religious education as a part of the basic but not the National Curriculum is important. It ensures that religious education has equal standing in relation to the core and other foundation subjects within a school's curriculum, but is not subject to *nationally prescribed* attainment targets, programmes of study, and assessment arrangements. However, a conference established by a local education authority under Schedule 5 of the 1944 Act to review a locally agreed syllabus, may recommend the inclusion of attainment targets, programmes of study and assessment arrangements in a *locally determined form* in their proposals. When drawing up an agreed syllabus, a conference should assume that there will be a reasonable time available for the study of religious education. Governing bodies of voluntary schools, and of grant-maintained schools which formerly had that status, may make similar provision in the religious education they provide according to their trust deeds as part of the school curriculum. The Secretary of State hopes that the possibility of doing so will be fully considered when an agreed syllabus is being reviewed, and when the governing bodies of such grant-maintained and voluntary schools are reviewing the provision they make for religious education.

Children with special educational needs and the National Curriculum

The Education Reform Act made it clear that in the view of the Secretary of State, all pupils, including those with special educational needs, should study the core and other foundation subjects of the National Curriculum to the maximum extent.

However, the Act does allow for the modification or disapplication of parts of the National Curriculum. If necessary, the programmes of study, the attainment targets, the requirements to study particular core or other foundation subjects, may all be disapplied. If suitable, sections of the National Curriculum may be modified rather than disapplied.

Some arrangements for disapplication of the National Curriculum may be upheld without Statements of special educational need where it is obvious that practical or physical work of certain kinds could be unsafe to pupils generally or injurious to the individual child.

In the case of individual children, a <u>Statement can disapply some or all of the National Curriculum</u> requirements if necessary. Any statement must indicate the modification to the National Curriculum which is proposed. If complete exemption from parts of the National Curriculum is considered necessary, full details need to be included in the Statement.

It is also possible for a headteacher to direct that the National Curriculum should be disapplied for a pupil on a temporary basis. The *DES Circular 15/89, section 19*, makes it clear that such arrangements may initially only be made for a period of six months. The direction may be one of the following two types:

1. *General directions:* A general direction may be made for *any* pupil who develops temporary problems, which would not be appropriate for a Statement (no longer than six months).
2. *Special directions:* These apply when a headteacher believes that the National Curriculum should be modified or disapplied in the case of an individual pupil because the LEA will need to assess the pupil for possible Statementing at a future date.

PUPILS WITHOUT STATEMENTS BUT WITH SPECIAL EDUCATIONAL NEEDS

The Warnock Report of 1978 concluded that up to 20 per cent of schoolchildren have special needs at some stage of their schooling. Headteachers, governors and LEAs have duties towards these children, even though they do not form part of the 2 per cent of children who are Statemented under the provisions of the 1981 Education Act.

It is important that all those who are responsible for 'special support' provision for these children should *keep parents fully informed of how the provisions of the National Curriculum are being applied to their children.*

The whole curriculum and the National Curriculum

At this stage it will be convenient to review what the National Curriculum Parliamentary Orders require by law and what they do not:

1. The Orders lay down the minimum requirements for each of the core and other foundation subjects. However, what is actually taught in schools *may go much wider*.

2. There will be opportunities for the *teaching of other subjects* and for a consideration of *cross-curricular study*.

3. The Orders do not require *any specific amount of time* to be spent on all or part of one of the programmes of study.

4. The Orders do not demand that a subject in the timetable should be provided *in a particular way*.

5. The Orders do not lay down *any teaching approaches or methods, teaching materials or textbooks.*

6. Until Orders for all foundation subjects come into effect, these subjects must be *taught for a reasonable time*. The term 'reasonable time' is not defined in the Education Reform Act.

7. There is no requirement that a pupil should *reach a particular level at a particular age.*

8. In the transitional stage of the National Curriculum, ie for the school year 1989–90, the targets and programmes of study for the core subjects will only apply to those children who have reached statutory school age by the beginning of the autumn term 1989. They will *not* apply to children who reach compulsory school age *during* the school year.

9. The Education Reform Act does not lay down which school subjects must be taken for GCSE, but it is envisaged that almost all pupils will continue to take the core subjects of the National Curriculum. In the case of foundation subjects which are not being taken for GCSE by a particular pupil, then National Curriculum arrangements will take account of the need for such pupils to continue with these subjects on a more limited basis.

SUBJECTS WHICH DO NOT FORM PART OF THE CORE OR OTHER FOUNDATION SUBJECTS OF THE NATIONAL CURRICULUM

Although in total the National Curriculum will cover a wide range of curriculum areas, it is clear that, for example, such areas as home economics, additional foreign languages, personal and social education, and topics covering moral beliefs and personal attitudes are not included as foundation subjects. At the later stages of secondary schooling account will also need to be taken of the implications of the Technical and Vocational Education Initiative (TVEI). Furthermore, although the National Curriculum suggests 'non-statutory' programmes of study, these only constitute examples which need to be related to locality and environment, the school catchment area, and its own overall organisation and ethos.

It has already been noted that the statutory Orders say nothing about styles of teaching and learning, although these factors themselves can be said to constitute a vital element of the received curriculum.

Primary level: the integration of the core subject targets

At this level the most significant difficulty with the presentation of the National Curriculum, in the context of the whole curriculum, lies in the fact that the attainment targets are presented in subject contexts whereas, as has been observed, the subject titles of the various elements of the whole curriculum are not normally 'filtered out' until a fairly late stage. For example, Key Stage 1 (5–7 year olds' requirements) in English, must emerge from a 'traditional' approach to language teaching and learning at the infant school level. Thus a typical session might start with the teacher encouraging the children to discuss class activities, visits, news, class stories and spontaneous incidents. Furthermore, individual children will frequently be asked to discuss their experiences with their teachers. The children's attempts to write may, at this stage, bear little resemblance to graphical conventions or word formations; their efforts are, however, strongly encouraged through praise and by asking them to read what they had 'written' to others.

Examples of the childrens' statements are then written out by the teacher: the children read their statements to the teacher and then copy out the statement. Reading elements of the session can be reinforced by 'word matching' activities and illustrations by the children. Finally, individual 'reading books' are compiled from a combination of the written work and the illustrations.

At Key Stage 2 (7–11 year olds), a variety of learning situations covering whole curriculum and National Curriculum requirements in an integrated approach, can arise from a scheme of work based on, for example, *The Wind in the Willows*. In this instance, (quoted in *Primary Schools: Some Aspects of Good Practice*, HMSO, 1987):

> the children entered imaginatively into the world of the book; they constructed a model of the riverbank, The Wild Wood and the houses of Rat, Mole and Badger, and Toad Hall. The children visited a local wood with their teacher and created a simulation of The Wild Wood in the classroom. This also provided the opportunity to introduce work on plans, maps and directions.

Such a topic can readily accommodate and integrate the National Curriculum core elements in the sense that the language element is covered through the literary choice of topic; mathematics elements arise through the necessity for measurement, estimates of size and scale, questions concerning the atmosphere and the use of, for example, a thermometer. Finally, scientific elements are covered through a consideration of the habitat and the occupants of the riverbank and their life-support systems.

These cross-curricular relationships in the core subjects were illustrated more formally in examples given in *A Framework for the Primary Curriculum* (NCC, 1989).

At Level I, cross-curricular language elements can be illustrated by a juxtaposition of what is required of children at each of the three core subject attainment targets:

English	*Science*	*Mathematics*
Participate as speakers and listeners in group activities, including imaginative play.	Describe and communicate observations, ideally through talking in groups, or by other means within the class.	Talk about own work and ask questions.
Use pictures, symbols or isolated letters, words or phrases to communicate meaning.	Be able to name or label the external parts of the human body and plants.	Create simple mapping diagrams showing relationships, read and interpret them.
Recognise that print is used to carry meaning, both in books and in other forms in the everyday world.		Count, read, write and order numbers.

At level 2, the elements are summarised thus:

English	*Science*	*Mathematics*
Respond appropriately to a range of more complex instructions given by a teacher and give simple instructions.	Ask questions and suggest ideas of the 'how' and 'why' and 'what will happen if' variety.	Ask and respond to the question, 'What would happen if ...?
Produce simple, coherent non-chronological writing.	Record findings in charts, drawings and other appropriate forms.	Describe current work, record findings and check results.
Structure sequences of real or imagined events coherently in chronological accounts.	Be able to keep a diary, in a variety of forms, of change over time.	Help to design a data collection sheet and use it to record a set of data leading to a frequency table.

Similarly, at Level 3:

English	*Science*	*Mathematics*
Relate real or imaginary events in a connected narrative which conveys meaning to a group of pupils, the teacher or another known adult.	Be able to give an account of an investigation.	Explain work being done and record findings systematically.

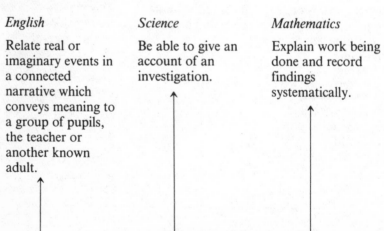

Level 3 *continued*

English	*Science*	*Mathematics*
Devise a clear set of questions that will enable selection and use of appropriate information sources and reference books from the class and school library.	Be able to retrieve and select text, number, sound or graphics stored on a computer.	Extract specific pieces of information from tables and lists. Enter and access information in a simple database.
Shape chronological writing, beginning to use a wider range of sentence connectives than 'and' and 'then'.	Be able to list the similarities and differences in a variety of everyday materials.	Place events in order of 'likelihood' and use appropriate words to identify the chance.

It must nevertheless be pointed out that there are limitations to the integrated topic approach — careful planning and recording of progress is vital, and the concept of a progressive subject approach must not be lost. This point was highlighted recently in an HMI report on geography and history at primary level, where it was commented that too little time was allocated to these subjects. A national survey found that no history whatsoever was taught in half of the primary schools that took part. It was reported that in these subject areas planning and teaching were often at an unsatisfactory level and assessment was either superficial or non-existent.

In practice, the most workable solution consists of a combination of both the topic and the subject approach to the curriculum. Thus in *Aspects of Primary Education* (HMI report, DES, 1989) it was commented that:

> each of these approaches had advantages and disadvantages; for example, sound links between science and other areas of the curriculum were made slightly more often when science formed part of topic work, while continuity and progression of scientific concepts and skills were more evident when the subject was taught separately.

Secondary level: the areas of experience and the construction of the whole curriculum

At secondary level the curriculum is usually presented in a style which reflects the National Curriculum foundation subject listings; however, at this level teachers are faced with the problem of finding time to instruct and implement a 'whole' curriculum to an extent which presents more practical difficulties than are imposed by the National Curriculum at primary level.

Contingent concerns such as the implications of mixed ability groupings, the special needs of ethnic minorities, and the future role of cross-disciplinary learning topics must all be taken into account, although a full consideration of these aspects of curriculum planning lies beyond the scope of this book. What must be remembered is that *there will always be limitations to any curriculum which is no more than a list of subjects.* Furthermore, the individual needs of the less able, the average and the very able pupil all deserve full planning consideration in curriculum building.

Most importantly, measures should be taken to avoid a subject lesson framework, all too common at secondary level, in which discussion and interpretation give way to 'written' lessons dominated by notes and summaries.

A vital omission in the Government's case for a National Curriculum was the lack of any underlying *theory* upon which a curriculum structure could be based. The justification for any subject being included in a timetable and the rationale of the teaching method itself, must lie beyond the 'subject titling' and find a *raison d'être* in its distinctive contribution to a particular *area of experience*. These areas of experience have often been described as functions of the 'nine adjectives', and this approach retains its validity today as a rule of thumb checklist for a whole curriculum or an 'entitlement curriculum' for every child.

The adjectives each describe a particular type of experience with a suggested classification as follows:

1. aesthetic and creative;
2. human and social;
3. linguistic and literary;
4. mathematical;
5. physical;
6. scientific;
7. technological;

8. moral;
9. spiritual.

Within each individual area of experience it is essential to ensure that each possible type of learning is given full consideration. The simplest distinction is commonly referred to as a difference in the meaning attached to the concept of 'knowledge'. Obviously a major aim of any curriculum is to impart knowledge. There is, however, a fundamental difference between *'knowledge that'* (ie the acquisition of information) and *'knowledge how'* (the acquisition of a skill). Additionally, quite a different type of knowledge rests in an understanding of ideas or concepts which are learned as abstractions rather than experiences.

If the rule-of-thumb guides to curriculum planning provided by the concepts of 'areas of experience' and 'elements of learning' are applied to the core and other foundation subjects of the National Curriculum, it is clear that the National Curriculum will in many ways match the concept of the whole curriculum in terms of a pupil's 'entitlement'. Thus the linguistic and literary aspects of the curriculum will be covered by the core subject of English; mathematical experiences will be covered by the mathematics core curriculum; the physical area of experience will be covered by the PE foundation subject; and the scientific area of experience clearly lies within the province of the core subject of science. Aesthetic and creative experiences can be subsumed under the headings of art and design and technology. Moral and spiritual areas of experience do not, however, feature as such in the foundation subjects of the National Curriculum.

Much language experience, as has been noted, will be covered by the English core subject of the National Curriculum, but this leaves indeterminate the area of experience represented by the general term of modern languages.

Indeed, the example of modern languages as a foundation subject of the National Curriculum at secondary level provides a useful instance of the operation of the rule of thumb, areas of experience approach to the curriculum. It is clear that modern languages justify a place in this approach, since the study of a modern language provides a 'unique' type of experience. However, the 'rule of thumb' does not provide any clue as to *which* modern language should be included in the curriculum. French has traditionally been the choice of modern language, both for historical reasons and due to the availability of teachers. It could, however, be argued that, from a practical point of view, the case for French filling the modern languages slot is becoming weaker as the 21st century approaches and French and English become increasingly interchangeable. This opens the way, in theory at least, for a modern foreign language other than French to be considered as satisfying both the areas of experience and the 'foundation subject' requirements. What is quite plain, however is that there is not a case for considering the inclusion of *more* than one modern language in the whole curriculum at main school secondary level.

The case of classical languages is a question for debate since it could be argued that the type of experience offered by this subject, although it is classed as a foreign language, differs in many ways from the experiences offered by the study of a modern foreign language.

A further example of the operation of the 'rule of thumb' can be demonstrated in the case of science. Scientific experience is of a unique type and therefore justifies its inclusion in the National Curriculum and the whole curriculum. However, such separate elements of science education as chemistry and physics, and to a lesser extent biology, cannot be considered for *individual inclusion* in the whole curriculum since they each offer similar types of experience. Hence, science is regarded in the National Curriculum and the whole curriculum as an *integrated subject.*

Personal and social education (PSE) does not rank as a foundation subject of the National Curriculum, yet this is a prime example of an 'area of experience' study which must be recognised and included in the whole curriculum. Thus the *National Curriculum Council Newsletter* of June 1989 declares that the teaching of PSE is perhaps the most important of the cross-curricular elements of the whole curriculum, since no component of the school curriculum can neglect its potential influence on PSE. Indeed, it is argued that PSE could act as a 'central thread linking all parts of the curriculum'. Although at primary school level the need for PSE can most readily be met through informal but close relationships with individual teachers, together with an involvement in the whole ethos of the school, there is a need for specific teaching at this level in relation to health education and similar issues.

At secondary level some PSE objectives can be achieved through the concept of 'work shadowing', enterprise situations and community service work. A defined area of PSE could also include topics such as multicultural issues and the implications of equal opportunities provision.

At the higher age levels in secondary schools, the whole curriculum will also need to relate to such initiatives as the TVEI, which has as its brief the need to react positively to the necessary preparation of young people for working life. To achieve these aims, the TVEI will need to support the National Curriculum and the whole curriculum in a number of ways. The possibilities were summarised in a joint statement from the National Curriculum Council and the Employment Department Training Agency in the summer of 1989. In this statement it was declared that TVEI would act as a supportive agency by:

- relating the whole curriculum to the world of work, encouraging the use of concrete and real examples;
- preparing young people for a highly technological society that is part of Europe and the wider world economy;
- providing direct opportunities to learn about work and the economy, for instance through work experience, work shadowing or projects in the community;
- promoting teaching and learning styles that encourage young people to be enterprising and creative, to solve problems and to work in teams;
- providing guidance and counselling, and opportunities to aid progression to continuing education and training.

Performance indicators (PIs) and the whole curriculum

Factors influencing the implementation of the whole curriculum may be summarised in performance indicator (PI) terms under the following headings, which could lead to a classification of 'best schools'. Such schools would exhibit:

- good leadership;
- clear aims and objectives, translated into classroom practice and carefully monitored;
- emphasis on high academic standards and the encouragement of all pupils to achieve to their potential;
- a relevant and orderly classroom atmosphere;
- good relationships with pupils and encouragement to express their own views;
- a coherent curriculum and a well-planned whole curriculum statement incorporating the elements of the National Curriculum;
- Concern for pupils' development as individuals in society, with a commitment by staff to their personal development;
- well-deployed staff, with experience and expertise, who receive appropriate development and training;
- suitable working accommodation and a stimulating environment;
- efficiently deployed and managed resources;
- good relationships with the community, parents and governors;
- a capacity to manage change and address problems logically.

Chapter 6

The Underlying Issues

Learning resources and the National Curriculum

The successful implementation of the National Curriculum depends not only on the availability of financial and human resources but also upon *learning resources* being deployed to the maximum advantage.

The National Council of Educational Technology (NCET) is in the process of producing learning packages which include computerised programmes and study kits dealing with aspects of the core foundation subjects of the National Curriculum. The use of off-air broadcast school programmes and LEA- and school-produced tape, slide and similar learning resources all need careful consideration and full planning in schemes of work in order to maximise the overall learning opportunities.

A principal learning resource will always centre around the purposeful use of books on an individual basis, a group or whole class basis and on a library approach basis. The printed word still remains the most powerful piece of information technology and the full development of this resource, notably in the context of the school library with its unrivalled learning opportunities potential, must become a prime factor in whole school planning.

The collections of books which collectively constitute library 'provision' may, in a small primary school, be physically housed in an entrance area, a corridor or a spare class space. Conversely, a large secondary school needs fully equipped and purpose-built accommodation which exploits modern technology and is under the purposeful control of a librarian. The organisation and positioning of the library are, of course, convenience factors: many schools with very inadequate provision make excellent use of their bookstock, while some schools with very good provision make superficial demands on this resource.

As noted, the implications of the National Curriculum require, more than ever, a *whole staff* approach to the topic of library book and non-book learning resources. Such a whole staff approach should ensure that library learning resources are well matched to learners' needs. They should be pleasant areas to be in and easy to get to, should be well equipped and have skilled staff who have the time to ensure that the needs of learners are met. They should be capable of developing the pupils' own capacities for self-learning in a learning resource environment, and should present, attractively, a well-chosen range of materials which relate effectively to the ages, abilities and interests of the learners. Finally, they should possess a funding system which takes full note of capital costing, current costing and obsolescence costing.

Information needs and the National Curriculum

The provisions of the Education Reform Act included an important section (Section 22) which entailed a full consideration of the information requirements which need to be met in order to secure the maximum effectiveness of the National Curriculum. The recipients of such information can be classed as follows:

1. *The School Pupils:* It is essential that children at school should fully understand what their programme of work consists of. They need to be aware of the objectives of the stage of the curriculum at which they are working and to know how they are progressing as individuals so that they can work to the full limit of their own potential.

2. *Parents:* Parents need detailed information about the educational arrangements and provisions of the school which their children will be attending. They also need information about the academic and general progress of their children. A 'spin-off' from arrangements which are well planned and presented will be the support and help which parents can offer to the school.

3. *Teachers:* As well as being responsible for the assessment and documentation of the achievements of their pupils, teachers need to possess sufficient information to enable them to plan curriculum progression, notably at the ages of school transfer.

4. *Headteachers:* Headteachers need to collate information about what is offered, in total, by their school, so that they can organise the overall curriculum in accordance with the statutory requirements. Additionally, they need full background information for their annual report to the school governors.

5. *Governing Bodies:* School governors need detailed information about the educational arrangements of their school to assist them to carry out their statutory duties, to prepare the annual governors' report and to provide information for the annual parents' meeting.

6. *LEAs:* Local Education Authorities need information in order to carry out their statutory duties under the Education Reform Act.

7. *Department of Education and Science:* The DES requires information in order that it can monitor the progress of the National Curriculum.

CURRICULUM INFORMATION
Each school is required to produce and publish details on curriculum topics as follows:

1. In the case of county and controlled schools, a summary of the governing body's statement of curriculum aims.
2. In the case of a voluntary aided or special agreement school, a summary of the governing body's statement of curriculum aims, or where none such exists, a statement to that effect.
3. A summary of the context and organisation of that part of the curriculum relating to sex education;
4. the time spent on teaching during each normal school day.
5. The dates of school terms and half-terms for the next school year.
6. A summary for each year group indicating how the school curriculum is organised and what it contains, including in particular how National Curriculum subjects and religious education are organised, what other subjects and cross-curricular themes are included in the curriculum for all pupils and what optional subjects are available and how choices among them are constrained.
7. A list of the external qualifications approved, under Section 5 of the Education Reform Act (ERA), for which courses of study are provided for pupils at the school.
8. The names of the syllabuses associated with the qualifications referred to in point 7, or where criteria for determining a syllabus are so approved, a statement to that effect.
9. A list of the external qualifications and names of associated syllabuses offered to those beyond compulsory school age.
10. Details of any careers education provided and the arrangements made for work experience.

11. Information about how to make a complaint according to arrangements established under Section 23 of the ERA.

Educational records of schoolchildren

The principal regulations governing the educational records of pupils can be summarised as follows:

1. *From September 1 1989* schools will be required to keep, and update at least once a year, *curricular records* on pupils, covering their academic achievements, other skills and abilities and progress in school. Other material, for example on the pupil's school attendance or family background, may be recorded, but that is not mandatorily required. This material and the curricular record together comprise the *educational record.*

2. *From September 1 1990* parents of pupils below the age of 18; pupils aged 16 or over; and schools and FE colleges considering a pupil for admission will be able to require disclosure of material on the educational record.

3. *From September 1 1989* schools will be required to transfer a pupil's educational record (except for ethnically based data, any report to a juvenile court and results of assessments of individual pupils) at the request of any school, or other education or training establishment to which the pupil transfers. Schools are already required, under regulations made in 1981, to transfer such records held on a pupil as the governors consider appropriate, upon request by the educational or training institution to which the pupil has transferred. (*DES News*, 239/89)

Records of Achievement and the National Curriculum

Record of Achievement schemes were set up on a pilot basis and evaluated by a Records of Achievement National Steering Committee in January 1989. After considering the report, the Government announced in August 1989 that regulations on reporting individual pupils' achievements would be introduced in 1990.

The introduction of the reports would be on a phased basis. Parents of pupils in the first groups of pupils to be covered would receive their reports in the summer of 1991.

The new government regulations, however, fell far short of the recommendations and aspirations of the National Steering Committee since it was stated that the reporting of pupils' achievements, particularly of those school years between the ends of each key stage, should be kept to a minimum. What was initially laid down by the regulations was a requirement that achievements should be reported in the National Curriculum subjects at the end of each key stage. However, the Junior Education Minister remarked, in August 1989, that in her view the regulations should provide for schools to report *each year* to parents on the progress of their child, and at the North of England Education Conference of January 1990, the Secretary of State referred to new draft regulations which would require a report at the end of each school year, showing the National Curriculum achievements of each child and the results of any public examinations.

The options system in secondary schools and the National Curriculum

Put in the simplest terms, the implementation of the National Curriculum at secondary level puts an end to the traditional option system at 14+ years. It may be said that pupils will be able to choose to study some National Curriculum subjects at a lower level, with a smaller time commitment. However, the majority of pupils committed to the ten subjects of the National Curriculum will wish to pursue them all to the limit of their ability. The needs of higher education at the post-16 level have exerted a dominance over secondary education since its state beginnings in 1902, and often curriculum systems have been devised which are designed to match the needs of the 14 per cent of pupils who progress to post-16 level full-time education rather than to the 86 per cent who may complete their full-time education at the statutory school leaving age of 16+ years.

The needs of the post-16 group of pupils obviously require full consideration at the main school planning level, and the demands, for example, of the individual sciences and higher education entry requirements for modern language or classical language study do pose questions.

In this connection three strategies deserve consideration:

1. A *postponement* of the majority of options until post-GCSE level.
2. An *introduction* to option subjects at pre-GCSE level through the study of cross-curricular topics.
3. An *extension* of the school day, or the introduction of 'out of school' study arrangements. It is worth pointing out that the

Government has proposed alterations to regulations concerning the length of the school day.

GCSE and the National Curriculum

Key Stage 4 of the National Curriculum which is intended to cover the age range 14–16 years will, of necessity, 'overlap' with the syllabuses, schemes of work and qualification arrangements of the 16+ GCSE examination.

This obvious fact led to considerable discussion between the School Examinations and Assessment Council, the National Curriculum Council and the Secretary of State. The Government finally took the view that the GCSE examination should form the principal method of assessment for the National Curriculum at Key Stage 4, commenting that the existence of two parallel systems would be 'a recipe for confusion'. In any necessary reappraisal of GCSE procedures and syllabuses, the Secretary of State maintained that there must be a balance between coursework and a final examination at the 16+ level. In this connection it was noted that at the present time performance in some GCSE subjects was assessed partly by coursework, some wholly by coursework and some entirely by examination.

It is to be expected that the majority of pupils will pursue the core curriculum subjects of the National Curriculum up to GCSE level and this will entail a consideration of how to match the GCSE grades A–G with the TGAT attainment scale 1–10, which has been accepted by the Government as the basis for the reporting of all National Curriculum attainments.

Three further major points require resolution before the introduction of Key Stage 4 reporting assessments in the core subjects, which are planned to come into effect in 1994:

1. In order to stretch the brightest pupils, the top of the GCSE scale (Grade A) should not be made to equate with Level 10 of Key Stage 4 of the National Curriculum. In other words, Level 10 of the National Curriculum would represent a higher level of attainment than the top grade of GCSE.
2. Conversely, for the weakest pupils, attainments at Levels 1–3 should not be equated with the lowest level of certification in GCSE (Grade G).
3. At the present time the Standard Achievement Tests are conceived of in terms of curricular element topics and used for assessment purposes only. GCSE subjects, on the other hand,

combine elements of teaching, learning and assessment. Some rationale for allowing a combination or 'evolution' of procedures will therefore be necessary.

Finally, a convergence of GCSE and the National Curriculum at Key Stage 4 must necessitate a revision of the draft orders for the attainment targets and programmes of study for this final key stage.

The National Curriculum and the 'sixth form'

As already remarked, the full implementation of the National Curriculum, with its requirements that the ten foundation subjects, together with religious education, must be studied by all pupils up to the age of 16 years, has important consequences for the traditional option systems, which generally come into operation at the 14+ level.

It is suggested that there is a general case for the postponement of a number of these options until after the GCSE and the National Curriculum Key Stage 4 levels have been reached. Deferral of choice until after GCSE has many advantages, not least being the increased likelihood of girls choosing post-GCSE individual science courses if the decision can be delayed until 16+.

A corollary of such an approach would be a rethinking of sixth form syllabuses at 'A' level, with a view to maintaining a breadth and balance of educational experience. A number of such initiatives are already under way, notably the City Technology Colleges approach to the question of sixth-form studies which, in some cases, includes the possibility of BTech diploma courses and study for the International Baccalaureate.

The Government has resolutely set its face against any 'dilution' of 'A' level standards; nevertheless the mould must be broken and the fundamental re-appraisal of the post-GCSE examination system will constitute an inexorable element in the progress of educational reform.

Professional reactions to the National Curriculum

The proposed introduction of a National Curriculum initially provoked a strong critical, and indeed hostile, reaction from the teaching profession. Although opinion veered gradually towards a general acceptance of the concept of a National Curriculum as the timetabled subject proposals became known, a deep unease continued to persist:

1. Although the declared objective of the educational reforms was

to raise standards, many teachers thought the implementation procedures were politically motivated to a high degree.

2. The supposition that the National Curriculum would automatically improve quality faced the criticism that what was being offered was a 'conveyer belt' system which was more likely to erode the features of quality which the teaching profession believed already existed in the majority of schools.

3. Particular anxiety and scepticism continued to be voiced on the topic of standard attainment tests. Here again, many teachers felt that the proposed testing arrangements would impose a severe constraint upon teaching situations, vastly increase the classroom workload and be open to considerable misinterpretation by the public.

4. The severest criticism was based on the fact that the expertise of teachers had not been sought and little information about the progress of the subject working parties was available. Indeed, the consultation documents did not reach many schools until well after the closing date for the receipt of comments.

5. Questions about the necessary in-service training of teachers and the problems of resourcing the National Curriculum figures largely in teachers' minds and the speed of the formal legislation of the National Curriculum proposals led to the criticism that the National Curriculum was being introduced in great haste.

The professional anxieties were well summarised by the comment that the implementation of the National Curriculum had been subject to 'minimal planning, consultation and development' (*TES*, 6 October 1989).

By the end of 1989, however, professional opinion discerned a return to reality: flamboyance had been faced with fact and the incoming Secretary of State swiftly put a stop on what would have been three major initiatives following the Education Reform Act:

1. The curricular innovators – namely the full-blown City Technology Colleges — were to be limited to a total number of 20, after an expenditure of public money in the region of £140 million. Originally industry had been thought as the major cost bearer; in the event the total contribution from outside sources amounted to approximately £50 million.

2. The introduction of teacher appraisal and assessment procedures was postponed indefinitely.

3. Plans for the national introduction of pupil Records of Achieve-

ment which had been expensively researched were virtually dismissed by the Department of Education and Science amid controversy as to whether such records should merely record the results of Standard Achivement Tests.

The future

In 1990, public and professional opinion began to veer towards a general acceptance of the desirability of increased rigour and some type of formalised targets for individual aspects of the school curriculum, together with a recorded assessment of the progress of each child.

Even at the primary stage, however, evidence has surfaced that the core subjects alone are already commanding the bulk of the school timetable. Indeed there remains a case for an initial restriction of the statutory sections of the National Curriculum to these basic subjects, with the addition only of religious education.

At the higher levels of the secondary school, some common ground must be found between the competing demands of the National Curriculum and those of the GCSE. Full-time education at post-16 levels will need to encompass demands for a 'start up' of the additional requirements of higher education which will have been held back by time-allocation restrictions imposed by National Curriculum foundation subjects. Indeed, a full rethink of post-16 full-time and part-time education, and the widening of access to further and higher education opportunities, are areas untouched by the Education Act reforms.

However, for the immediate future the whole enterprise has been overshadowed by the increasing shortage of trained and experienced professionals, at all levels and in all subjects. This is resulting in a situation which cannot but eclipse even the most realistic hopes for the full implementation of a National Curriculum.

Appendix I

Summary of Attainment Targets in the Core Subjects at Level 4*

English

(AT 1) (i) Give a detailed oral account of an event, or something that has been learned in the classroom, or explain with reasons why a particular course of action has been taken, or express a personal view.

(ii) Ask and respond to questions in a range of situations with increased confidence.

(iii) Take part as a speaker and listener in a group discussion or activity, commenting constructively on what is being discussed or experienced.

(iv) Participate in a presentation.

(AT 2) (i) Read aloud expressively, fluently and with increased confidence from a range of familiar literature.

(ii) Demonstrate, in talking about a range of fiction and poetry which they have read, an ability to explore preferences.

(iii) Demonstrate, in talking about stories and poems, that they are developing their abilities to use inference, deduction and previous reading experience.

(iv) Find books or magazines in the class or school library by using the classification system, catalogue or database and use appropriate methods of finding information, when pursuing a line of enquiry.

(AT 3) (i) Produce, independently, pieces of writing showing evidence of a developing ability to structure what is written in ways that make the meaning clear to the

* Note: The formal statements of each Attainment Target (AT) are given on pages 34–57.

reader; demonstrate in their writing that they have understood the use of sentence punctuation.

(ii) Write stories which have an opening, a setting, characters, a series of events and a resolution and which engage the sympathy and interest of the reader; produce other kinds of chronologically organised writing.

(iii) Organise non-chronological writing for different purposes in orderly ways.

(iv) Begin to use the structures of written Standard English and begin to use some sentence structures different from those of speech.

(v) Discuss the organisation of their own writing; revise and redraft the writing independently in the light of that discussion.

(AT 4)   (i) Spell correctly, in the course of their own writing, words which display other main patterns in English spelling.

Science

(AT 1)   (i) Raise questions in a form which can be investigated.

     (ii) Formulate testable hypotheses.

   (iii) Construct 'fair tests'.

   (iv) Plan an investigation where the plan indicates that the relevant variables have been identified and others controlled.

    (v) Select and use a range of measuring instruments, as appropriate, to quantify observations of physical quantities, such as volume and temperature.

   (vi) Follow written instructions and diagrammatic representations.

  (vii) Carry out an investigation with due regard to safety.

 (viii) Record results by appropriate means, such as the construction of simple tables, bar charts, line graphs.

   (ix) Draw conclusions from experimental results.

    (x) Describe investigations in the form of ordered prose, using a limited technical vocabulary.

(AT 2)   (i) Be able to recognise similarities and differences both within and between groups of plants and animals.

      (ii) Understand the key factors in the process of decay (temperature, microbes, compactness, moisture) and how this is important in the re-use of biological material in everyday life.

     (iii) Understand that plants and animals can be preserved as fossils in different ways.

(AT 3)   (i) Be able to name the major organs and organ systems in flowering plants and mammals.

      (ii) Know about the factors which contribute to good health and body maintenance, including the defence systems of the body, balanced diet, oral hygiene and avoidance of harmful substances such as tobacco, alcohol and other drugs.

     (iii) Understand the process of reproduction in mammals.

     (iv) Be able to describe the main stages of flowering plant reproduction.

(AT 4)   (i) Be able to measure variations in living organisms.

(AT 5)   (i) Know that some waste materials can be recycled.

(AT 6)   (i) Be able to make comparisons between materials on the basis of simple properties: strength, hardness, flexibility and solubility.

      (ii) Be able to relate knowledge of these properties to the everyday use of materials.

     (iii) Know that solids and liquids have 'weight' which can be measured and, also, occupy a definite volume which can be measured.

     (iv) Understand the sequence of changes of state that results from heating or cooling.

     (v) Be able to classify materials into solids, liquids and gases on the basis of their properties.

(AT 7)   (i) Know that when a chemical reaction occurs, new materials are formed.

      (ii) Know that an important feature of manufacture is the conversion of raw materials, by chemical reactions, into useful products.

(AT 8)   (i) Be able to use their developing ideas about the constitution of matter and relate them to everyday examples involving changes of state and solubility.

(AT 9)   (i) Be able to measure temperature, rainfall, wind speed and direction: be able to explain that wind is air in motion.

(ii) Know that climate determines the success of agriculture and understand the impact of occasional catastrophic events.

(AT 10)   (i) Understand that the movement of an object depends on the size and direction of the forces exerted on it.

(ii) Understand that the greater the speed of an object the greater the force and/or time that is needed to stop it and understand the significance of this for road safety.

(iii) Understand that things fall because of a force of attraction towards the centre of the Earth.

(iv) Be able to recognise that weight is a force, and know that it is measured in newtons.

(AT 11)   (i) Be able to construct simple electrical circuits.

(AT 12)   (i) Know about the range of uses of microelectronic devices in everyday life.

(ii) Be able to detect and measure environmental changes using a variety of instruments.

(AT 13)   (i) Understand that energy is essential to every aspect of human life and activity.

(ii) Know that there is a range of fuels which can be used to provide energy.

(iii) Understand that energy can be stored, and transferred to and from moving things.

(iv) Be able to measure temperature using a thermometer.

(v) Be able to give an account of changes that occur when familiar substances are heated and cooled.

(AT 14)   (i) Know that it takes time for sound to travel.

(AT 15)   (i) Know that we see objects because light is scattered off them and into our eyes.

(ii) Know that light travels in straight lines and use this to explain the shapes and sizes of shadows.

(AT 16) (i) Know that the phases of the moon change in a regular and predictable manner.

(ii) Know that the solar system is made up of the sun and planets, and have an idea of its scale.

(iii) Understand that the sun is a star.

(AT 17) (i) Be able to give an account of some scientific advance, for example in the context of medicine, agriculture, industry or engineering, describing the new ideas and investigation or invention and the life and times of the principal scientist involved.

Mathematics

(AT 1) (i) Select the materials and the mathematics to use for a task; plan work methodically.

(ii) Record findings and present them in oral, written or visual form as appropriate.

(iii) Use examples to test statements or definitions.

(AT 2) (i) Read, write and order whole numbers.

(ii) Understand the effect of multiplying a whole number by 10 or 100.

(iii) Use, with understanding, decimal notation to two decimal places in the context of measurement.

(iv) Recognise and understand simple everyday fractions.

(v) Recognise and understand simple percentages.

(vi) Understand and use the relationship between place values in whole numbers.

(AT 3) (i) Know multiplication facts up to 10×10 and use them in multiplication and division problems.

(ii) Using whole numbers, add or subtract mentally two 2-digit numbers; add mentally several single-digit numbers; without a calculator add and subtract two 3-digit numbers, multiply a 2-digit number by a single-digit number and divide a 2-digit number by a single-digit number.

(iii) Solve addition or subtraction problems using

numbers with no more than two decimal places; solve multiplication or division problems starting with whole numbers.

(AT 4) (i) Make use of estimation and approximation to check the validity of addition and subtraction calculations.
(ii) Read a calculator display to the nearest whole number.
(iii) Know how to interpret results on a calculator which have rounding errors.

(AT 5) (i) Apply strategies, such as doubling and halving, to explore properties of numbers, including equivalence of fractions.
(ii) Generalise, mainly in words, patterns which arise in various situations.

(AT 6) (i) Understand and use simple formulae or equations expressed in words.

(AT 7) (i) Know the conventions of the coordinate representation of points; work with coordinates in the first quadrant.

(AT 8) (i) Understand the relationship between units.
(ii) Find areas by counting squares, and volumes by counting cubes, using whole numbers.
(iii) Make sensible estimates of a range of measures in relation to everyday objects or events.

(AT 9) (i) Select the materials and the mathematics to use for a task; plan work methodically.
(ii) Record findings and present them in oral, written or visual form as appropriate.
(iii) Use examples to test statements of definitions.

(AT 10) (i) Understand and use language associated with angle.
(ii) Construct simple 2-D and 3-D shapes from given information and know associated language.

(AT 11) (i) Specify location by means of coordinates (in first quadrant) and by means of angle and distance.

     (ii) Recognise rotational symmetry.

(AT 12)   (i) Specify an issue for which data are needed; collect, group and order discrete data using tallying methods with suitable equal class intervals and create a frequency table for grouped data.

     (ii) Understand, calculate and use the mean and range of a set of data.

     (iii) Interrogate data in a computer database.

(AT 13)   (i) Create a decision tree-diagram with questions to sort and identify a collection of objects.

     (ii) Construct, read and interpret a bar-line graph for a discrete variable (where the length of the bar-line represents the frequency).

     (iii) Construct and interpret a line graph and know that the intermediate values may or may not have a meaning.

     (iv) Construct and interpret a frequency diagram choosing suitable class intervals covering the range for a discrete variable.

(AT 14)   (i) Understand and use the probability scale from 0 to 1.

     (ii) Give and justify subjective estimates of probabilities in a range of events.

     (iii) List all the possible outcomes of an event.

Other Foundation Subjects — Examples from Interim Reports

History

Five profiles or attainment targets are proposed for history:

AT 1: Historical understanding displaying a sense of time and place.

AT 2: Understanding points of view and interpretations.

AT 3: Acquisition and enquiry.

AT 4: Analysis and evaluation of a wide range of sources.

AT 5: Organisation and expression.

By way of example, the descriptions of attainments expected at Level 1 are given below. At this level the targets will obviously be integrated into the general infant school framework rather than being regarded as separate subject items.

(AT 1)   (i) Understand the ideas of past and present in terms of:
               (a) some clear differences between 'then' and 'now';
               (b) a few objects and pictures widely spaced chronologically;
               (c) simple family trees and the sequence of generations.
      (ii) Understand that material surroundings and possibilities were different in the past.

(AT 2)   (i) Understand that there exist different views about the past.

      (ii) Understand the distinction between real and imaginary people.

(AT 3)   (i) Acquire and discuss information obtained by listening to or reading simple historical stories, including historical fiction or direct accounts of past events, and poetry, and by participating in dramatic activities.

      (ii) Gather information (which they understand to have come from the past) from a range of visual sources and physical remains.

(AT 4)   (i) Understand that traces of the past are evidence of it.

      (ii) Recognise and discuss the difference between reality and fantasy.

     (iii) Discuss, compare, question and speculate on historical sources in order to extract information from them.

(AT 5)   (i) Describe, using IT where appropriate, aspects of the past:
  (a) orally or in writing;
  (b) through drama or dance or music;
  (c) visually;
  (d) graphically.

Geography

Eight profiles or attainment targets are proposed for geography:

AT 1: The Home area and region.

AT 2: The United Kingdom.

AT 3: World geography (I).

AT 4: World geography (II).

AT 5: Physical geography.

AT 6: Human geography.

AT 7: Environmental geography.

AT 8: Geographical skills.

As examples of the operation of the attainment targets in geography, instances of Level 2 attainments are given as follows:

AT 1   Be able to identify and name types of familiar features found in the vicinity of their school.

AT 2   Know that people in the UK live in a variety of different environments (eg a town, a suburb, a village, the countryside).

AT 5   Know that there are patterns in the weather related to seasonal changes, and be able to record the weather over a short period of time pictorially and in words (eg use weather charts to record wet, dry, hot, cold, windy period).

AT 6   Understand that people belong to different countries (eg UK, France, Japan, Soviet Union, USA).

AT 7   Know how some common materials and sources of energy are obtained (eg quarrying, mining, forestry, farming, rivers).

AT 8   Record actual or imaginary territories in 'map' form.

Technology (final report)

Four profiles or attainment targets are suggested for Technology:

AT 1: Identifying needs and opportunities.

AT 2: Generating a design proposal.

AT 3: Planning and making.

AT 4: Evaluating.

Details of the content of the four attainment targets at Level 3 are given, by way of example, as follows:

(AT 1)   (i)   Starting with something familiar, use their knowledge and the results of investigations to identify needs and opportunities for a design and technological activity.

(ii) Develop and clarify their ideas about possible needs and opportunities through discussion with those involved.

(AT 2)   (i)   Record how they have explored different ideas about design and technological proposals to see how realistic they are.

(ii) Use information about materials, people, markets and processes, and from other times and cultures, to help in developing their ideas.

(iii) Make a design proposal by selecting from their ideas and giving reasons for their choices.

(iv) Apply knowledge and skills to select ways of realising the different parts of their design.

(v)   Use drawings and modelling including annotated drawings and working models to develop their design proposals.

(AT 3)   (i)   Choose resources for making by using their knowledge of the characteristics of materials and components.

(ii) Use a range of hand tools and equipment, appropriate to the materials and components, with some regard for accuracy and quality.

(iii) Consider constraints of time and availability of resources in planning and making.

(iv) Improvise within the limits of materials, resources and skills when faced with unforeseen difficulties.

(AT 4)   (i)   Discuss their design and technological activities with teachers and others, taking into account how well they have met the needs of others.

(ii) Comment on the materials and processes used and how the task was tackled.

Summary of the Basic Ideas of the National Curriculum

1. *The subjects to be taught*
   All children must study the ten subjects which constitute the National Curriculum. These subjects are:

   - English
   - mathematics
   - science
   - technology (and design)
   - history
   - geography
   - music
   - art
   - physical education
   - a modern foreign language (at secondary level, ie 11–16 years)

2. *The 'core subjects'*
   Of the ten subjects to be studied at school, three subjects are designated as basic or core curriculum subjects. These are:

   - English
   - mathematics
   - science

   These three core subjects, combined with the seven other subjects, are termed the foundation subjects of the National Curriculum.

   Religious knowledge: This subject is not designated as a core or foundation subject but, following the 1988 Education Reform Act, it is stipulated that religious knowledge must form an essential part of the whole school curriculum. (See pages 16, 67–8).

3. *Attainment targets*

In each subject a range of objectives is stated. These objectives describe what children at each stage of their schooling should be able to achieve. These lists of achievements are known as attainment targets.

4. *Programmes of study*

Parliamentary Orders also include descriptions of possible programmes of study which are designed to enable children to reach the attainment targets.

5. *Assessments*

The performance of each child will be assessed by a combination of internal and external markings at four specific ages during the school life of the child. These ages are 7 and 11 for the primary years of schooling and 14 and 16 for the secondary years of schooling.

6. *Key stages of schooling*

The content of the National Curriculum is regarded as being composed of four key stages which correspond to the age groupings between the four assessment ages. Thus:

- Key Stage 1 covers the 5–7 age group
- Key Stage 2 covers the 7–11 age group
- Key Stage 3 covers the 11–14 age group
- Key Stage 4 covers the 14–16 age group

7. It is not intended that the subject statements in the parliamentary Orders should cover the whole of the curriculum of a school. It is specifically stated in the 1988 Act that there would be time for other subjects to be studied. Each school will decide for itself how many other subjects can be fitted into the school timetable. It is also possible that some subjects may be studied on a cross-curricular basis.

8. *Special educational needs*

It is envisaged that children with special educational needs will, as far as circumstances permit, follow the National Curriculum. This is in order to ensure that these children will have the widest educational opportunities that can be offered to them. For children with statements of special educational needs the requirements of the National Curriculum will be deferred for one year and will therefore be introduced in the Autumn of 1990. Additionally, parts of the National Curriculum may be judged not to apply to some children with special educational needs, either temporarily or on a more permanent basis.

9. *Information to parents*

All schools are required to publish relevant information in the prospectus of the school and in the governing body's annual report on the topic of the total curriculum of the school. Parents will receive from the school, information about how their child has fared in the national tests and assessments. These national assessments will be on a ten-point scale which is intended to cover the whole range of a child's achievement from the age of 5–16. Thus Levels 1–3 will correspond to the school ages 5–7. An average child can be expected to have achieved approximately Level 4 by the age of 11 years. By 14 years, Levels 5 or 6 should have been achieved. By the age of 16 an average child may have reached Level 7. A below average child may complete his or her schooling at around Level 6, while a very bright child may achieve the top level, ie Level 10. The emphasis is on a rate of progress which is suitable for each individual child, and on a steady progression rather than a static level of achievement.

DES Press Notices Referring to the National Curriculum

List of Abbreviations

AT   Attainment Target
CC   Core Curriculum
DES   Department of Education and Science
ERA   Education Reform Act
GCSE   General Certificate of Secondary Education
HMI   Her Majesty's Inspector of Schools
KS   Key Stage
LEA   Local Education Authority
NC   National Curriculum
NCC   National Curriculum Council
SACRE   Standing Advisory Council on Religious Education
SAT   Standard Assessment Test
SEAC   School Examinations and Assessment Council
SLA   School Leaving Age
SOS   Secretary of State
SSA   Statutory School Age
TGAT   Task Group on Assessment and Testing
TVEI   Technical and Vocational Education Initiative

Useful Addresses

DES free documents   may be obtained from:

> DES Publications Despatch Centre (PDC)
> Honeypot Lane
> Canons Park
> Stanmore
> Middlesex HA7 1AZ
>
> Tel: 01-952 2366

DES priced documents   may be ordered through HMSO bookshops
or from:

> HMSO Publications Centre
> PO Box 276
> London SW8 5DT

National Curriculum Council documents   are ordered through:

> National Curriculum Council
> 15/17 New Street
> York YO1 2RA
>
> Tel: 0904 622533

School Examinations and Assessment Council publications
are available from:

> Information Centre
> School Examinations and Assessment Council
> Newcombe House
> 45 Notting Hill Gate
> London W11 3JB
>
> Tel: 01-229 1234

Further Reading

National Curriculum documents

Assessment and Testing	*Task Group Report*	DES, 1988
	Digest	DES, 1988
Technology	*Technology 5–16* (Final Report)	NCC, 1988
English:	*English 5–11* (Consultation Report)	DES, 1989
	English 5–16 (Final Report)	NCC, 1989
Geography:	*Geography 5–16* (Interim Report)	DES, 1989
History:	*History 5–16* (Interim Report)	DES, 1989
In-service:	*Developing INSET Activities*	NCC, 1988
Introduction:	*An Introduction to the National Curriculum*	NCC, 1989
Mathematics:	*Mathematics 5–16* (Final Report)	NCC, 1989
Primary phase:	*A Framework for the Primary Curriculum*	NCC, 1989

Science: *Science 5–16* NCC, 1989
(Final Report)

HM Inspectors of Schools have published detailed discussion documents on the foundation subjects of the National Curriculum as follows:

1. *English from 5 to 16* (1986) (Second edition), HMSO.

2. *Mathematics from 5 to 16* (1987) (Second edition), HMSO.

3. *Music from 5 to 16* (1985) HMSO.

4. *Geography from 5 to 16* (1986) HMSO.

5. *Modern Foreign Languages from 5 to 16* (1987) HMSO.

6. *Craft, Design and Technology from 5 to 16* (1987) HMSO.

7. *History from 5 to 16* (1988) HMSO.

Index